Web-Scale Workflow and Analytics

Series Editor
M. Brian Blake

More information about this series at http://www.springer.com/series/14343

Iman Saleh

Formalizing Data-Centric Web Services

Iman Saleh
Intel Corporation
Santa Clara, CA, USA

ISSN 2365-8347   ISSN 2365-8355 (electronic)
Web-Scale Workflow and Analytics
ISBN 978-3-319-36810-8   ISBN 978-3-319-24678-9 (eBook)
DOI 10.1007/978-3-319-24678-9

Springer Cham Heidelberg New York Dordrecht London

Printed on acid-free paper

Springer International Publishing AG Switzerland is part of Springer Science+Business Media (www.springer.com)

To my mother Yousria and my late father Saleh

Preface

Web services are reusable software components that make use of standardized interfaces to enable loosely coupled business-to-business and customer-to-business interactions over the Web. In such environments, service consumers depend heavily on the service interface specification to discover, invoke, and synthesize services over the Web. Data-centric Web services are services whose behavior is determined by their interactions with a repository of stored data. A major challenge in this domain is interpreting the data that must be marshaled between consumer and producer systems. Current standards for specifying Web services, such as the Web Services Description Language (WSDL) and Representational State Transfer (REST) APIs, only specify a service operation in terms of its syntactical inputs and outputs. These standards do not provide a means for specifying the underlying data model, nor do they specify how a service invocation affects the data. The lack of data specification potentially leads to erroneous use of the service by a consumer. In this book, we propose a formal contract for data-centric Web services. A formal contract is a set of machine-readable assertions that specify the behavior of a piece of software. The goal is to formally and unambiguously specify the service behavior in terms of its underlying data model and data interactions. We address the specification of a single service, a flow of services interacting with a single data store, and also the specification of distributed transactions involving multiple Web services interacting with different autonomous data stores. We use the proposed formal contract to decrease ambiguity about a service behavior to fully verify a composition of services and to guarantee correctness and data integrity properties within a transactional composition of services.

Santa Clara, CA   Iman Saleh

Acknowledgment

I'd like to thank Gregory Kulczycki and M. Brian Blake for their help with the work presented in this book.

Contents

Chapter 1
Introduction

Abstract In the past years, the Web has evolved from an information sharing medium to a wide-scale environment for sharing capabilities or *services*. Currently, URLs not only point to documents and images, but are also used to invoke services that potentially change the state of the Web. The Web provides services for booking airline tickets, purchasing items, checking the weather, opening a bank account and many other activities. Web services also play a major role in the Internet of Things (IoT) vision where connectivity and interoperability of wearable devices and sensors is a main challenge. Web services and APIs are used by IoT systems to connect devices to the Internet; a process characterized by high level of data processing. Service-Oriented Architecture (SOA) is a key player in implementing these systems as it enables exposing applications as reusable, interoperable, network-accessible software modules commonly known as Web services.

1.1 Background

Current SOA technologies provide platform-independent standards for describing these services. Service providers follow these standards to advertise their services' capabilities and to enable loosely coupled integration between their services and other businesses over the Web. A major challenge in this domain is interpreting the data that must be marshaled between consumer and producer systems. Although freely-available services are often specified using the Web Services Description Language (WSDL) [1] for Web services, the Representational State Transfer (REST) [2] or the Web Application Description Language (WADL) [3], these standards specify a service operation only in terms of its syntactical inputs and outputs; they do not provide a means for specifying the underlying data model, nor do they specify how a service invocation affects the data. These challenges surrounding data specification can lead consumers to use a service erroneously.

As detailed in Fig. 1.1, in order for a service consumer to produce the input messages that must be used to invoke a web service, she must interpret natural language specifications (annotated as A) and formulate messages as specified with WSDL specifications (annotated as B). We suggest that there is some logical data model and business rules (annotated as D) that exist between the interface-based messages

© Springer International Publishing Switzerland 2015   1
I. Saleh, *Formalizing Data-Centric Web Services*, Web-Scale Workflow
and Analytics, DOI 10.1007/978-3-319-24678-9_1

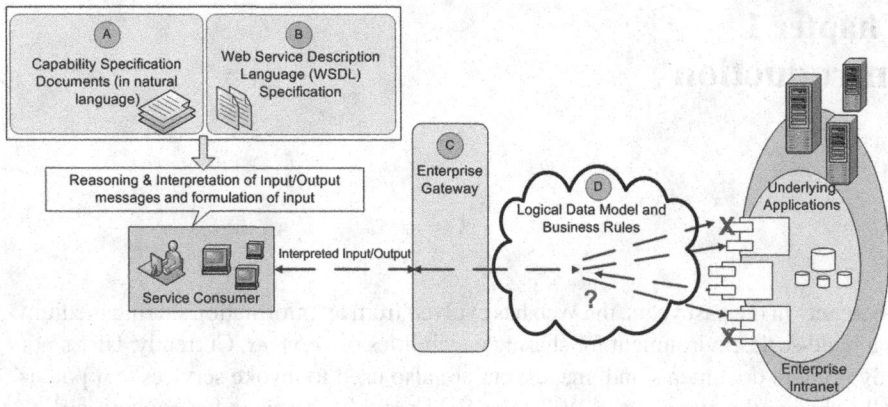

Fig. 1.1 Data specification challenges within the service-oriented architecture

and the underlying concrete software applications. With the existing service-based specifications, the definition of this model and rules is not well represented.

We believe that aspects of formal specifications as represented in software engineering practices could provide solutions for effectively specified data-centric Web services. Formal methods allow for more rigor than process-oriented languages, such as the Business Process Execution Language for Web Services (BPEL4WS) [4] and the semantic-based specification languages such as the Web Services Ontology Language (OWL-S) [5].

Although application logic varies significantly from one service to another, we are able in this work to capture commonalities and use them to create a generic formal model that describes a service's data functionalities. We then use the formal model to create a data contract for a service. The contract is a set of formal assertions which describes the service behavior with respect to its interaction with the data. The contract also exposes data-related business rules. Since our model is based on formal methods and design-by-contract principles, it provides a machine-readable specification of the service. This facilitates automatic analysis, testing, and reasoning about the service behavior. We show how our model can be useful in decreasing ambiguity, verifying the correctness of integration of services and also in proving data integrity properties in service-based transactions.

Practically, Web services promote a paradigm where new software applications are built by dynamically linking online services. Changes in the service's implementation and its underlying data schema are likely to occur throughout a service's lifetime. The service consumer requires a guarantee that this service evolution will not break his/her applications. This is where the formal contract comes into play by exposing some obligations that the service provider has to maintain by the underlying implementation such that the service consumers are not affected. This is crucial in the case of Web services since the service is invoked remotely and binding is done at runtime while the service implementation and the underlying data infrastructure remain under the provider's control.

1.2 Observations

Major online organizations today, such as Amazon [6], PayPal [7] and FedEx [8], provide services for users and consumers. They also allow third-party vendors to resell their services. Both cases require precise and complete specification of service offerings. Several online discussions demonstrate the challenges faced by these organizations and others while describing their data-centric Web services. Some consumers' feedback include:

> *I have met a problem when I was trying to get the sales rank of digital cameras using the web service. It showed me pretty different sales ranks from what I saw through Amazon Website. For instance, a certain type of camera ranks No. 2 on their website, but ranked No. 8 when I call it through the Web service. I guess this problem is because the ranks are different since products are searched through different category...But I am not sure.* [9]

> *There are some items which have an image on the detail page at Amazon, but I can't retrieve the image location with the Web service request...* [10]

> *Can someone explain the precise distinction between 'Completed' and 'Processed' [as the output of a PayPal payment transaction service]?* [11].

> *You can find information about Web Services on the FedEx Site. But when you look at the [Developer Guide], it's two pages long and incredibly vague* [12].

These comments and many others indicate the confusion of service consumers due to unspecified data interactions and hidden business rules. The current standards for specifying Web services fail to capture effectively these interactions and rules. Informal documentation is currently used by service providers to fill this gap by providing natural language descriptions of service capabilities. However, natural language documentation is often ambiguous and imprecise which leads to more confusion about how to use a service correctly.

1.3 Scope of the Work

Web services interacting with a source of data are becoming increasingly common and used by developers over the Web as well as within enterprises' boundaries. These services include e-commerce services, news, travel reservations, banking services and others. The main goal of our research is to formally model and specify the data aspect of these Web services, as it is overlooked by current standards for specifying Web services. The formal specification enables verification of service behavior. We use formal methods and design-by-contract techniques to achieve this goal.

We consider data-centric Web Services whose behavior is determined by their interactions with a data store. Our approach is applicable to both structured and semi-structured data stores such as relational and object-oriented databases, spreadsheets, semi-structured text documents, and XML files. These data stores exhibit some structural organization of the data either by a defined data schema like in relational databases or by including schema information with the data like in XML files.

In this book, we show how the formal specification and verification of data-centric Web services can be facilitated by exposing a formal data contract. We develop a formal model for an abstract source of data and develop a contracting framework for data-centric Web services based on the abstract model. We then investigate how the data contract can be used to specify a service, a composition and a service-based transaction and verify some behavior properties. We can split our main hypothesis into the following hypotheses that we validate throughout our work.

While our model is applicable to any data-centric application, it is most useful in the case of Web services for the following reasons:

- Testing and debugging a Web service is much costlier and time-consuming than a local method call. Service providers may restrict the number of calls, or charge the consumer for each call, so trial and error may not be an option [13, 14].
- Web services can be exposed to a very wide range of clients that use different technologies [13]. So it is important for service providers to be able to unambiguously define the service behavior to simplify error and exception processing. Service consumers should be able to distinguish between functional and non-functional causes of errors when invoking services.
- With the increasing need for automation, Web services will soon be accessed directly by software agents, applications, and IoT devices and sensors rather than by human beings [15]. A relevant example is the REST-based Constrained Application Protocol (CoAP) enabling machine-to-machine applications for IoT [16]. A machine-readable data contract is an essential ingredient to fulfill this promise since it enables automated reasoning about the service behavior.

1.4   Evaluations

Hypothesis I: The proposed contracting approach decreases the level of ambiguity about a Web service behavior in terms of its underlying data interactions and expected output under different input conditions.

Validation Approach: We use our model to specify a simplified version of the *ItemSearch* service which searches for items within Amazon.com product catalog given a set of search filters (Chap. 8). We then consider a case study where the *ItemSearch* service is used by a Web search engine to crawl data from Amazon database. We use this case study to evaluate our model's success in decreasing the level of ambiguity about the service behavior. Our evaluation is based on the observation that the more queries the crawler has to try to retrieve the same set of data records, the more ambiguous the service behavior. Consequently, we consider the total number of possible input combinations (queries) as an indication of the level of ambiguity of the service specification. Our goal is to minimize the total number of input combinations by only considering the relevant ones. Filtering out invalid or redundant input combinations is done based on the crawler understanding of the exposed data contract.

Hypothesis II: Formal code specification and verification facilitates the discovery of implementation errors at design time. These errors cannot be detected using a non-verifying compiler. The effectiveness of different levels of specifications in detecting errors can be quantified.

Validation Approach: We investigate the impact of various levels of formal specification on the ability to statically detect errors in code. Our goal is to quantify the return on investment with regards to the effectiveness of identifying errors versus the overhead of specifying software at various levels of detail. We conduct an experiment where we use 13 common algorithms and data structures implemented using C# and specified using Spec# [17] (Chap. 9). We mutate the code by injecting errors using a fault injection tool and then run the mutated code through a code verifier. The effectiveness of the specification is measured by the number of errors detected at each level of specification.

Hypothesis III: Our proposed contracting approach facilitates the discovery of implementation errors in data-centric Web services at design time. These errors cannot be detected using a non-verifying compiler. The effectiveness of different levels of specifications in detecting errors can be quantified.

Validation Approach: Similar to hypothesis II, we investigate the impact of various levels of formal specification on the ability to statically detect errors in an implementation. Through experimentation, we add our model and formal contract to a set of data-centric Web services implementing a book rental application. The experiment is applied on 17 data-centric functionalities implemented using C# and specified using Spec# (Chap. 10). We mutate the code by injecting errors using a fault injection tool and then run the mutated code through a code verifier. The effectiveness of the specification is measured by the number of errors detected at each level of specification.

Hypothesis IV: Our proposed contracting approach enables the specification and verification of correctness properties in a composition of services.

Validation Approach: We use our model and contracting approach to expose heavyweight specification for a flow of services and we present a full flow verification based on the exposed specification (Chap. 5). We also demonstrate the feasibility and practicality of applying our model by implementing it using three of the state-of-the-art specification and verification languages (Chap. 7).

Hypothesis V: The proposed contracting approach enables verifying the data integrity within an ACID transaction that spans multiple autonomous Web services. ACID (atomicity, consistency, isolation, durability) is a set of properties that guarantee that database transactions are processed reliably.

Validation Approach: We consider a scenario where an e-commerce Website developer uses FedEx to ship orders to customers and uses PayPal to implement the electronic payment functionalities (Chap. 6). The scenario is implemented by integrating the corresponding Web services from the two service providers. The developer would like to consider this scenario as an ACID transaction and would hence like to ensure the "all-or-nothing" property. Consequently, if an error occurs within the transaction, a compensating action should be applied to undo any database update. For example, if the FedEx shipment processing service fails, the e-commerce

Website should invoke a refund service against PayPal database to compensate the customer's payment.

We investigate how the data contract of individual services can be used to verify data integrity properties. As an example, the integration should guarantee that on successful completion of the transaction, the customer PayPal account is charged exactly the item cost plus the shipping cost while FedEx account is charged only the shipping cost.

1.5 Outline

This book is organized as follows: Chap. 2 highlights some of the problems with the current state of data-centric Web services and presents background fundamental to our work. Chapter 3 reviews the research related to the formal specification and verification of data centric Web services. Chapter 4 formally describes the CRUD-based data model we developed and indicates how it is used in the context of Web services. Chapter 5 demonstrates how to use our framework to reason formally about a sequential Web-service composition, and Chap. 6 demonstrates how to use our framework to reason formally about a transactional composition. Chapter 7 shows how the framework can be adapted to work with state-of-the-art formal reasoning tools. Chapters 8–10 give empirical evaluations of the potential impact of our model. Chapter 8 gives an example of how a formally specified Web service can facilitate deep-Web searches. Chapters 9 and 10 show experiments in which formally specified systems allow significantly better detection of errors without ever running the program. Chapter 9 shows the experiment performed with common algorithms while Chap. 10 shows a similar experiment performed with services specified using our data model. The application of the design-by-contract approach to Web services is discussed in Chap. 11. Finally, conclusions are discussed in Chap. 12.

Chapter 2
Background

Abstract This chapter presents basic concepts that we will be referring to throughout this manuscript. Readers who are familiar with one or more of the presented concepts can safely skip the corresponding sections.

2.1 Web Services

Web Services are software systems designed to support interoperable machine-to-machine interaction over a network [18]. They are modular software components with interface descriptions that can be published, located, and invoked across the Web. They provide a form of remote procedure call (RPC) over the Internet based on existing protocols and using widely accepted standards (e.g., XML) [19]. Web Services are designed with reuse in mind and can be described as 3C-style components [20] that include Concepts (interfaces), Contents (implementations), and Contexts.

Different technologies have emerged to support the Web Services model. WSDL (Web Services Description Language) [1] is a standardized way to describe service structures (operations, messages types, bindings to protocols, and endpoints) using XML. Recently, RESTful [2] Web services have emerged as a simpler design model where services are invoked using HTTP requests.

When compared to distributed object models like CORBA [21], Web Services have the following distinguishing characteristics [19]:

- They are intended to be used in a global scope, not just in local organizational contexts.
- Due to a loose coupling between components, they provide a better support for ad-hoc distributed computing.
- Web Services are easy to use since they rely on infrastructure readily available in commonly used operating systems.
- The use of transport protocols such as HTTP makes Web Services easier to access through firewalls of organizations.

Web Services are nominally stateless. A Web Service does not remember information or keep state from one invocation to another. Services should be independent, self-contained requests, which do not require the exchange of information

© Springer International Publishing Switzerland 2015

I. Saleh, *Formalizing Data-Centric Web Services*, Web-Scale Workflow and Analytics, DOI 10.1007/978-3-319-24678-9_2

or state from one request to another, or depend on the context or state of other services. When dependencies are required, they are best defined in terms of common business processes, functions, and data models, not implementation artifacts (like a session key) [22].

2.2 Formal Methods

The encyclopedia of Software Engineering [23] defines formal methods as follows:

> *Formal Methods used in developing computer systems are mathematically based techniques for describing system properties. Such formal methods provide frameworks within which people can specify, develop, and verify systems in a systematic, rather than ad hoc manner.*

A method is formal if it has a sound mathematical basis, typically given by a formal specification language. This basis provides the means of precisely defining notions like consistency and completeness. It provides the means of proving that a specification is realizable, proving that a system has been implemented correctly with respect to its specification, and proving properties of a system without necessarily running it to determine its behavior [24].

In our work, we use Hoare-style specification. Hoare-style specification employs preconditions and postconditions to specify the behavior of a method [25]. If P and Q are assertions and Op is an operation, then the notation:

```
operation Op
      requires P
      ensures Q
```

denotes that P is a precondition of the operation Op and Q is its postcondition. If the precondition is met, the operation establishes the postcondition. Assertions are formulas in predicate logic that evaluate to either true or false.

In the following subsections, we present some of the formal methods concepts that we are using in our work.

2.2.1 Lightweight Versus Heavyweight Specification

A lightweight specification is typically used to verify only some behavior properties. Consider, for example, a stack push operation. The operation takes an object and adds it to the top of a stack. The following is a lightweight specification for the push operation:

```
public interface Stack{
    ...
    push(Object x)
      ensures this.length() == #this.length() + 1
    ...

}
```

The '#' symbol is used to denote the value of a variable before the invocation of the operation. The postcondition specifies that the length of the stack is incremented by one after the *push* operation. It doesn't specify which object is inserted into the stack or even where the object is inserted. Lightweight specification is typically used in runtime assertion checking [26] or to enhance compile-time static checking [27].

Heavyweight specification is intended to be a complete mathematical description of a component's behavior. A heavyweight specification requires a mathematical model for all types. To apply heavyweight specification to the push example, we need a mathematical model for the stack. We can model the stack as a mathematical string. For example, the empty string (< >) represents a stack with no elements, the string <a> represents a stack with exactly one element, a, and the string <a, b, c> represents a stack with three elements, whose first element is the top of the stack [28]. The following postcondition uses this mathematical model to specify the behavior the *push* operation.

```
public interface Stack{
    ...
    push(Object x)
      ensures this == <#x> o #this // String concatenation
    ...

}
```

The above postcondition specifies that the object is appended at the front of the string which corresponds to the top of the stack. Given this heavyweight specification we can verify not only the change in the stack length (as in the case of lightweight specification), but also the change in the stack structure after the operation completes.

Heavyweight specification includes all clauses and assertions necessary for complete verification, such as abstraction relations, representation functions, loop invariants, and decreasing clauses [23] in addition to class invariants, preconditions and postconditions.

2.2.2 Symbolic Reasoning

The symbolic reasoning technique was introduced in [29] as a natural way to generate the proof obligations required in formal verification. It can be seen as a generalization of code tracing, where object values are represented symbolically rather than concretely [28]. We will be using symbolic reasoning to prove that a composition of services is implemented correctly with respect to the advertized data contract. In our proofs, we will depend on sub-contracts exposed by the individual services in a composition.

The following description of the symbolic reasoning technique is based on [28]. Natural reasoning [29] about code correctness can be viewed as a two-step process:

1. Record local information about the code in a symbolic reasoning table, a generalization of a tracing table.
2. Establish the code's correctness by combining the recorded information into, and then proving, the code's verification conditions.

Step 1 is a symbol-processing activity no more complex than compiling. It can be done automatically. Consider an operation *Foo* that has two parameters and whose body consists of a sequence of statements (see Fig. 2.1). You first examine stmt-1 and record assertions that describe the relationship which results from it, involving the values of x and y in state 0 (call these x_0 and y_0) and in state 1 (x_1 and y_1). You similarly record the relationship which results from executing stmt-2, i.e., involving x_1, y_1, x_2, and y_2; and so on. You can do this for the statements in any order because these relationships are local, involving consecutive states of the program.

We use a symbolic reasoning table at step 1. There are four columns in a symbolic reasoning table—the *state*, the *path condition*, the *facts*, and the *obligations*. The *state* serves the same purpose as it does in the tracing table. The *path condition* column contains an assertion that must be true for a program to be in that particular state. The *facts* contain assertions that are true assuming that the state has been

Fig. 2.1 Relationships in symbolic reasoning

```
operation Foo (x, y)
  requires
    pre [x, y]
  ensures
    post [#x,#y, x, y]
  procedure Foo (x, y) is
   begin
    // state 0
    stmt-1
    // state 1
    stmt-2
    // state 2
    stmt-3
    // state 3
    stmt-4
    // state 4
   end Foo
```

reached, and the *obligations* are assertions that need to be proved before a program can move to the next state.

Step 2 of natural reasoning involves combining the assertions recorded in step 1 to show that all the obligations can be proved from the available facts. This task can be done in a semi-automatic way using computer-assisted theorem proving techniques.

In the case of specifying Web services, a statement corresponds to a Web service call. A state is represented by the values of inputs and outputs in addition to model variables representing the underlying data store. In other words, the data model can be considered as a global variable whose value constitutes a part of the program state.

2.3 Transaction Basics

From a database point of view, a transaction is a logical unit of work that contains one or more statements. A transaction is an atomic unit. The effects of all the statements in a transaction can be either all applied to the data or all undone. This is known as the "all-or-nothing" proposition. In this work, we are considering ACID transactions [30]. The ACID attributes refers to Atomicity, Consistency, Isolation and Durability. The exact meanings of these attributes can be described as follows:

- Atomicity: The transaction's changes to the application state are atomic. A transaction has an "all-or-nothing" characteristic as stated before. Either all the changes occur or none of them happen.
- Consistency: A transaction is a correct transformation of the application state. The actions of a transaction do not violate any integrity constraints; the transaction is a "correct program". The applied integrity constraints depend on the particular application [31].
- Isolation: Multiple transactions occurring at the same time do not impact each other's execution. In other words, each transaction is unaware of other transactions executing concurrently in the system. Note that the isolation property does not ensure which transaction will execute first, merely that they will not interfere with each other.
- Durability: When a transaction completes successfully, the changes it did to the application state have to be permanent and have to survive any kind of failure. Durability is ensured through the use of database backups and transaction logs that facilitate the restoration of committed transactions in spite of any subsequent software or hardware failures.

Our proofs for the correctness of a Web Service-based transaction in Chap. 6 address both the atomicity and consistency aspects. Isolation and durability are assumed to be handled by the underlying data management infrastructure.

Chapter 3
Literature Review

Abstract Unlike software components operating within an enterprise, the Web services model establishes a loosely coupled relationship between a service producer and a service consumer. Service consumers have little control over services that they employ within their applications. A service is hosted on its provider's server and is invoked remotely by a consumer over the Web. In such settings, it is important to establish a contract between the service provider and the service consumer. We study the modeling and formalization of such contract to capture not only a service input and output, but also its data interactions and side effects, if any.

3.1 Modeling and Specification of Web Services

Our work in modeling and specifying data is applicable to software components in general. We focus however on Web services, as a form of modular and reusable software components, since they introduce peculiar reuse challenges. Unlike software components operating within an enterprise, the Web services model establishes a loosely coupled relationship between a service producer and a service consumer. Service consumers have little control over services that they employ within their applications. A service is hosted on its provider's server and is invoked remotely by a consumer over the Web. In such settings, it is important to establish a contract between the service provider and the service consumer. The contract establishes a set of obligations and expectations. These obligations can be functional, specifying the service operations in terms of its pre/postconditions. They can also be non-functional pertaining to legal, security, availability and performance aspects. The peculiar challenges introduced by Web Services are discussed in [32] and are summarized in Sect. 1.3.

Semantic approaches have gained a lot of attention in Web Services community as a way to specify service capabilities. A survey of semantic Web service techniques can be found in [22]. Semantic techniques are based on description logic. Description logic is used to build ontologies to annotate the input and output parameters for Web services and to semantically define service capabilities. The W3C OWL-S standard for semantically describing Web services is an example of such an approach [5]. Description logic supports the definition of concepts, their properties and relationships. The reasoning tasks supported by description logic include instance checking, i.e. validating whether a given individual is an instance of a specified concept; relation checking, i.e. validating whether a relation holds between two instances; and the subsumption, i.e. validating whether a concept is a subset of another concept [33]. This makes techniques based on description logic suitable for solving problems related to the automatic discovery and composition of services as these problems require matching between a semantically-annotated user query and a semantically-specified Web service.

In contrast, our work is based on formal methods which support verification of correctness of a computer program. Formal methods are suitable for solving problems related to correctness and verifying that a service complies with its advertized formal specification.

From a software engineering perspective, the semantic technique and formal methods techniques are complimentary as they address software validation and verification problems, respectively. While a semantic-based approach can validate that a service or a composition of services match a user query, a formal method approach can verify that the service or composition of services is implemented correctly with respect to that user query.

As a relevant example, the authors in [34] present a model for a data providing services. A data providing service is a read-only service that provides access to one or more possibly distributed and heterogeneous databases. The service's main functionality is to retrieve data from a data store based on an input query. Their approach is based on semantic technologies to facilitate the automatic discovery of services by applying ontological reasoning. In order to deal with schemas and data heterogeneity, they suggest describing data sources as RDF[1] views over a shared mediated schema. Specifically, the local schema of each data source is mapped to concepts of a shared OWL ontology, and its terms are used to define RDF views describing the data sources in the mediated schema [34]. Their approach is useful in matching a service with a user query based on ontology-based reasoning. They do not, however, tackle correctness issues or reasoning about the service side-effects.

Similar to our work, the authors of [35] apply design-by-contract principles to Web services. They use an ontology-based approach to attach a legal contract to a service. The authors also propose a semi-automatic process for contract negotiation that ensures that the service execution complies with the advertised contractual terms. Formal and informal Service-Level Agreements (SLAs) are also commonly used as part of a service contract to specify measurable performance metrics like service availability and response time. W3C standards like The Web Services Policy specification [36] provides a framework for attaching quality-of-service attributes to a service interface.

---

[1] Resource Description Framework, an official World Wide Web Consortium (W3C) Semantic Web specification for metadata models.

While non-functional contracts have gained a lot of attention lately [35–40], we advocate the importance of specifying functional aspects of a data-centric Web service related to its underlying data interactions. To our knowledge, this aspect has been so far neglected by current work in service contracting. A consumer integrating a data-centric Web service within an application may be oblivious of side effects on the data that are relevant to her/his application. This potentially leads to unintended consequences from using the service. To remedy this situation, we propose that a service provider exposes a set of data obligations. A service has to comply with these obligations regardless of internal code or schema updates. The obligations in our case are represented as a set of data manipulation functionalities.

Our work builds on traditional efforts for formally specifying relational databases. A comprehensive survey of the work in that area can be found in [41]. These efforts aimed at deriving relational database programs from formal specification. This implies exhaustively specifying the database schema, constraints and operations and using the specification to derive database transactions. While our work borrows from the methodology of that approach, there are three fundamental differences that arise from the fact that we are specifying Web services as black box components. First, our goal is to expose a data contract and not to build the service logic from the specification. Hence we do not aim at exhaustively specifying the underlying database schema, but rather to abstract this schema in a model that is exposed as part of the service interface. The model in our case should actually be abstract enough to avoid revealing unnecessary or proprietary details about the underlying data, while still being useful in writing the contract terms. Secondly, the work in that area focused on applications running against one database and hence an implicit assumption is that the database integrity is maintained by the underlying Database Management System (DBMS). Consequently, the consistency of the data after a transaction completion is guaranteed and compensation actions are not specified by this work. In our case of specifying data-centric Web services, we are not specifying transactions over one database based on the same rationale. We are however interested in transactions spanning more than one database, where it is the responsibility of the service consumer to guarantee integrity while having no control on the underlying DBMSs. This can be seen as a special case of a distributed transaction that performs a set of logically-related updates against autonomous databases with no mediator to ensure data integrity across these databases. This is typically the case when services are composed and consumed over the Web by agents or human developers. It is hence the responsibility of the service consumer to ensure the integrity of the data after executing a distributed transaction. The specification in this case is used to ensure and verify these integrity properties. Finally, our model is not specific to relational databases. A data source in our case can be a database, a CSV file, an RSS feed, a spreadsheet, or other type of data store. We therefore built our model while avoiding constructs that are too specific to relational databases such as cascade updates or table joins.

3.2   Modeling and Specification of Data-Centric Processes

The work in [42–44] addresses the formal analysis of an artifact-centric business process model. The artifact-based approach uses key business data, in the form of "artifacts", as the driving force in the design of business processes. The work focuses on three problems; reachability, avoiding dead-ends, and redundancy. Both this work and ours depend on specifying databases. The difference however is that the business process is concerned by modeling states and state transition. Consequently, specifying the database from a process perspective is an NP-Complete problem as the data can have infinite number of states and state transitions. The mentioned work tries to make simplifying assumptions in order to make the problem tractable. In our work, we are specifying and reasoning about stateless Web services by modeling the state of the relevant system. We consider the underlying data store as a global variable that we are including as part of the formal specification of a service. We are concerned with reasoning about the changes of that global variable between a service request and response. We do not attempt to specify all states of a data store as we focus on correctness and verification of data-related side-effects after a service call.

Another related work presented in [45] handles the specification of interactive Web applications and focuses on specifying Web pages and user actions. The proposed data model incorporates temporal constructs to specify browsing paths between pages and application behavior in response to user actions such as clicking a button or browsing through hyperlinks. The approach is hence useful in verifying properties like page reachability and the occurrence of some events. Again, this approach is working from a process perceptive and hence an input-boundedness restriction is assumed to guarantee that the verification operation can be done in polynomial time.

3.3   Transaction Management Protocols for Web Services

Research in transactions planning has recognized the evolvement of Web Services as an industry standard to implement transactional business processes. The OASIS Business Transactions Protocol (BTP) [46] and the Web Services Transactions (WS-Tx) [47, 48] specification are the two major efforts in this area. These protocols define interactions between the service consumer and the service provider to ensure that they agree on the outcome of a transaction. It is assumed that compensation transactions are implemented to undo updates upon transaction failures.

While these techniques are meant to ensure database integrity, they are all based on the assumption that service interactions against the database are well defined and known before planning a transaction. They also assume that service developers will follow protocol guidelines while implementing their data-centric Web Services and that a mediator exists to coordinate between service providers. These assumptions are only valid when all services belong to a specific business domain or implemented within the same enterprise with strict conventions. On the Web however, services are typically combined from different providers that potentially employ different implementation conventions and practices. The assumption of a mediator becomes impractical for the Web setting. Moreover, many hidden business rules related to data manipulation may lead to incorrect transaction outcome even if transaction management measures are in place.

Since our model formally specifies the data behavior of an individual service by exposing a data contract, it enables the verification of the outcome of the transaction based on the individual contracts of participating services. Our model also helps in identifying unambiguously the exact compensation steps upon transaction failure. Global data integrity is hence guaranteed at the design time of the transaction.

3.4 Formal Specification and Verification of Data-Centric Web Services

Prior to this book, the author has worked on applying formal methods techniques to Web Services as part of a doctoral dissertation research [49]. The vision and motivation behind that work was first introduced in [50]. In [51], the core model for specifying data behavior is presented along with the potential of using formal specification to decrease ambiguity about service behavior. In [52], we presented experimentation to explore the role of using formal specification for writing error-free code. Building on that work, the experiments presented in [53] apply the proposed formal techniques to data-driven applications and in [54] to, more specifically, the transacational database applications. The implementation of the proposed model and specification is discussed in [55]. In this book, previous research is synthesized and potential applications are presented. We discuss here the formal modeling of data-centric Web services and show, using practical examples, the use of the formal model in the specification and automatic verification of service compositions.

Chapter 4
Modeling and Specification
of a Data-Centric Web Service

Abstract In order to formally specify a data-centric Web service, we need first to model the data managed by a service. The model should accommodate different data infrastructures and should support the formal definition of data-related business rules. The model should be also flexible enough to support different levels of abstraction. In the remainder of this manuscript, we will use the term Web service to refer to an operation that is invoked remotely over the Web. While a WSDL file can contain the description of more than one operation. We choose to refer to each operation as a Web service for simplicity.

4.1 Generic Data Model

We model a data source as set of entities where each entity is a set of records. In addition to a unique record identifier (key), a record can have zero or more attributes. We view this model as a common denominator of many popular data models that we surveyed [56–58] including mainly the relational and object-oriented modeling of databases, and some earlier efforts for formally specifying databases [41, 59]. We adapt the CRUD (Create-Read-Update-Delete) [60] model to include functional descriptions of the basic data operations. We implement our model as a generic class to facilitate its understanding by programmers of Web services. The model is shown in Listing 4.1.

The *Read* operation is supported in our model by two functions; *findByKey* and *findByCriteria*. The *findByKey* function takes a data model and a key value and returns a record whose key value matches the input key. The *findByCriteria* function takes a data model and set of filtering values for each attribute type in the model. It returns a set of records such that an attribute value of a returned record is a member of the corresponding input filtering set.

Our generic model class can be used as the basis for a reusable JML [26] or Spec# [17] specification class to model different data-centric services.

© Springer International Publishing Switzerland 2015   19
I. Saleh, *Formalizing Data-Centric Web Services*, Web-Scale Workflow
and Analytics, DOI 10.1007/978-3-319-24678-9_4

```
class GenericDataModel

    attribute entity₁: Set(GenericRecord₁)
    attribute entity₂: Set(GenericRecord₂)
    ...
    attribute entityₙ: Set(GenericRecordₙ)

    operation GenericRecordᵢ findRecordByKey(key: GenericKeyᵢ)
        requires (GenericKeyᵢ is the key for GenericRecordᵢ )
        ensures  result.key = key and result in this.entityᵢ
                 or  result = NIL

    operation Set(GenericRecordᵢ) findRecordByCriteria(values₁: Set(Tᵢ₁),
                                                       values₂: Set(Tᵢ₂),
                                                       ...
                                                       valuesₙ: Set(Tᵢₙ))
        requires (Tᵢⱼ is the type of the jᵗʰ attribute of GenericRecordᵢ )
        ensures ∀rec in result, rec.attrⱼ in valuesⱼ
                     and result in this.entityᵢ

  operation GenericDataModel createRecord(gr:GenericRecordᵢ)
      requires this.findRecordByKey(gr.key) = NIL
      ensures result.entityᵢ = this.entityᵢ U gr
          and ∀j ≠ i, result.entityⱼ = this.entityⱼ

  operation GenericDataModel deleteRecord(key: GenericKeyᵢ)
      requires this.findRecordByKey(key) ≠ NIL
      ensures result.entityᵢ = this.entityᵢ - this.findRecordByKey(key)
          and ∀j ≠ i, result.entityⱼ = this.entityⱼ

  operation GenericDataModel updateRecord(gr:GenericRecordᵢ)
      requires findRecordByKey(gr.key) ≠ NIL
      ensures result.entityᵢ = deleteRecord(gr.key).createRecord(gr)
          and ∀j ≠ i, result.entityⱼ = this.entityⱼ
end GenericDataModel
```

```
class GenericRecord

      attribute key: T_key
      attribute attr₁: T₁
      attribute attr₂: T₂
      ...
      attribute attrₙ: Tₙ

end GenericRecord
```

Listing 4.1 The generic data model class

Using the proposed model, a developer of a data-centric Web service can specify its data-behavior by following these steps:

1. Abstracting the service underlying data model as set of records, and identifying their attributes' types.
2. Implementing the service data model as a class using our generic data model as a template (Listing 4.1).
3. Annotating the data model class with invariants that define any data constraints or business rules.
4. Annotating the service interface with formal specifications that are defined in terms of the data model and data functionalities defined in step 2.

4.2 Example: Amazon's Item Search Service

Amazon provides a collection of remote services for e-commerce tools. As of January 2015, Amazon services are by more than a million customers. We will use our model to specify a simplified version of the *ItemSearch* service which searches for items within Amazon product catalog given a set of search filters. The service is described as follows:

Service signature	Data types

ItemInfo[] ItemSearch
(searchIndex: CatString,
    keywords: String,
    minPrice: Float
    maxPrice: Float
    author: String
    artist: String
    title: String
    availability: AvailString
    merchant: String
    sort: SortString)
	CatString: Enum of {Books,
	CD, DVD, All}
	AvailString: Enum of {Available}
	SortString: Enum of {price, -price}
	ItemInfo: Array of [itemId: Integer,
	    detailPageURL: String,
	    title: String,
	    author: String,
	    artist: String]

We used the service documentation available at [9] and our own testing of the service to guess the underlying data schema and constraints, and specified the service behavior accordingly. We model the service data as a set of records of type *ItemRecord*. Listing 4.2 shows our model implemented as the *ItemSeacrhDataModel* java class that is based on our template class defined earlier. *ItemSeacrhDataModel* supports the same data operations as our template class. We have, however, omitted their definition in Listing 4.2 to avoid repetition. The data constraints and business rules are defined as class invariants. The corresponding JML notation is listed in Appendix A. For example, the *ItemRecord* class invariant at line 8 states that a record whose category is either *CD* or *DVD* cannot have a non-null *author* attributes.

Our model can be used to represent relationships between entities. For example, if each item is related to a *merchant* record, the following can be added to the *ItemRecord* class to represent this relationship:

```
attribute merchnatID: Integer
```

And, the following invariant is added to the *ItemSearchDataModel* class:

```
invariant (∀ ItemRecord irec; ∃ MerchantRec mrec; irec.merchantID
== mrec.id)
```

Finally, Listing 4.3 is the service specification based on the defined data model. The service preconditions and postconditions are enclosed in requires and ensures clauses, respectively. The '#' symbol prefix denotes the value of

```
class ItemSearchDataModel

      attribute itemEntity: Set(ItemRecord)

end ItemSearchDataModel
```

```
class ItemRecord

      attribute key: Integer
      attribute category: { Book, CD, DVD }
      attribute merchantName: String
      attribute author: String
      attribute artist: String
      attribute title: String
      attribute price: Float
      attribute stockLevel: Integer

      invariant (category = CD or category = DVD) ⇒ author = NIL
      invariant (category = Book) ⇒ artist = NIL
      invariant stockLevel ≥ 0
      invariant price ≥ 0
      invariant (stockLevel > 0) ⇒ merchantName ≠ NIL
      invariant title ≠ NIL

end ItemRecord
```

Listing 4.2 The *ItemSearch* data model class

```
1  requires minPrice ≥ 0 and maxPrice ≥ 0 and minPrice ≤ maxPrice
2  ensures result.length ≥ 0
3  // The following specification variables are assumed: isdm: ItemSearchDataModel
4  // authors, artists, titles, merchants: Set(String)
5  // searchIndices: Set(CatString)
6  // prices: Set(Float)
7  // stockLevels: Set(Integer)
8  // Specifying the results in terms of the service inputs and the defined model
9  ensures ∀i, 1 ≤ i < result.length,
10 result[i] ∈ { [rec.key, "http://www.amazon.com"+rec.key, rec.title, rec.author,
11        rec.artist] | rec ∈ isdm.findRecordByCriteria(searchIndices, merchants,
12                              authors, artists, titles, prices, stockLevels)}
13 // Case 1: searching by keywords in the CD and DVD categories
14 ensures #keywords ≠ NIL and (#searchIndex = CD or #searchIndex= DVD) ⇒
15    {DVD,CD} ∈ searchIndices and #keywords ∈ artists and #keywords ∈ titles
16 // Case 2: searching by keywords in the Books category
17 ensures #keywords ≠ NIL and #searchIndex = Books ⇒
18       Book ∈ searchIndices and #keywords ∈ authors and #keywords ∈ titles
19 // Case 3: searching by keywords in all categories of items
20 ensures #keywords ≠ NIL and #searchIndex = All ⇒
21                         {Book, DVD, CD} ∈ searchIndices and #keywords ∈ titles
22 // Case 4: searching by title in the Books category
23 ensures #title ≠ NIL and #searchIndex = Books ⇒
24                         Book ∈ searchIndices and #title ∈ titles
25 // Case 5: searching by author in the Books category
26 ensures #author ≠ NIL and #searchIndex = Books ⇒
27                         Book ∈ searchIndices and #author ∈ authors
28 // Filtering results by the min and max prices
29 ensures #minPrice ≠ NIL ⇒ ∀ Float v ∈ prices, v ≥ #minPrice
30 ensures #maxPrice ≠ NIL ⇒ ∀ Float v ∈ prices, v ≤ #maxPrice
31 // Filtering results by availability
32 ensures #availability = Available ⇒   Z⁺ ∈ stockLevels
33 ensures #availability = NIL ⇒   {0} U Z⁺ ∈ stockLevels
34 // Filtering results by the merchant name whose default value is "Amazon"
35 ensures #merchant ≠ NIL ⇒   #merchant ∈ merchants
36 ensures #merchant = NIL ⇒    "Amazon" ∈ merchants
37 // Results are sorted based on the value of the sort input
38 ensures #sort=price ⇒ ∀i,1≤i<result.length,result[i].price ≤ result[i+1].price
39 ensures #sort=-price ⇒ ∀i,1≤i<result.length,result[i].price ≥ result[i+1].price
```

Listing 4.3 The *ItemSearch* data contract

a variable before service execution. The variable result denotes the service output. We define a specification variable *isdm* of type *ItemSearchDataModel*. Additionally, a group of specification variables (lines 4–7) are used to denote data filters. For example, the assertion at line 17:

```
ensures (#keywords ≠ NIL) and (#searchIndex = Books) =>
    Book ∈ searchIndices and #keywords∈ authors and #keywords ∈
titles
```

denotes that when the input keywords is provided, and the *searchIndex* input is set to Books, the search is done for items with category equal to Book and either the title or the author is matching the keywords. For the sake of simplicity, we assume the service searches for an exact match between the keywords and the title/author. The sets *searchIndices*, authors and keywords are used in line 11 as the input filtering sets to the *findByCriteria* function. Lines 13–27 represent different search scenarios (search by keywords, by title, etc.). Lines 28–36 represent further filtering criterion based on input parameters. Lines 37–39 specify that when the sort input is set to *price*, the resulting items are sorted in ascending order by the item price and when sort input is set to *-price*, the results are sorted in descending order.

It should be noted that, while the model provides the necessary constructs for full specification of the data model and data interactions, it is up to the service developer to decide on the sophistication level of the specification. This flexibility ensures that our model is applicable under different time and cost constraints.

Chapter 5
Specification and Verification
of a Composition of Services

Abstract In this chapter, we show how our model can be used to specify and verify a sequential flow of data-centric Web services. A sequential flow of services is essentially made up of a number of individual services that are executed in a specific order and are integrated by means of sequential composition, loops and conditional statements. This is a traditional service composition problem where a service consumer integrates the functionalities of two or more services in order to construct a new service that provides a more complex functionality. The challenge that we are addressing here is how to guarantee that the integration will have the intended final effect on the underlying data.

5.1 Problem Description and Assumptions

Using our proposed contracting framework, we assume that each service in the flow exposes a data contract that specifies its data behavior. The service consumer (integrator) trusts the correctness of the individual contracts and uses them to understand the data behavior of the whole flow of services. The contracts also enable proving correctness properties at the design-time of the services' composition. In our approach, we are assuming that data sharing and concurrency issues are typically handled by the data management system maintained by the service provider. This enables us to model the data as a global variable, and still be able to apply modular verification techniques on a composition of services with two or more services sharing the same data infrastructure.

We apply our specification and verification approach to PayPal Express Checkout flow [61]. The Express Checkout flow is used by e-commerce website developers to implement electronic payments through PayPal. The flow is implemented as a composition of three services. We provide individual contracts for each service in the composition and a global contract that represents the intended behavior of the flow. We also provide formal proofs of some correctness properties that have to be maintained by the composition of services. To the best of our knowledge, no current specification of Web services supports formal verification of correctness of data properties in a service composition.

© Springer International Publishing Switzerland 2015   25
I. Saleh, *Formalizing Data-Centric Web Services*, Web-Scale Workflow
and Analytics, DOI 10.1007/978-3-319-24678-9_5

5.2   Proposed Methodology

Figure 5.1 shows how our proposed contract-based framework supports modeling and contracting of a composition of services. In the figure, solid lines represent verification steps, while dotted lines represent reference relationships.

Assuming a service consumer is building an application by composing services from different providers as shown in the figure, our framework ensures the correctness of the composition and data consistency by applying the following steps for advertizing and using Web services:

1. A service provider abstracts the data source(s) into a formal data model, discussed later. The model hides the data design and implementation details. Figure 5.1 shows that Service Provider A may choose between two different database implementations that comply with Data Model A.
2. The service provider annotates the service with a data contract that formally specifies the data requirements and service side-effects. The data contract is published along with the service WSDL file. It is the provider's responsibility to

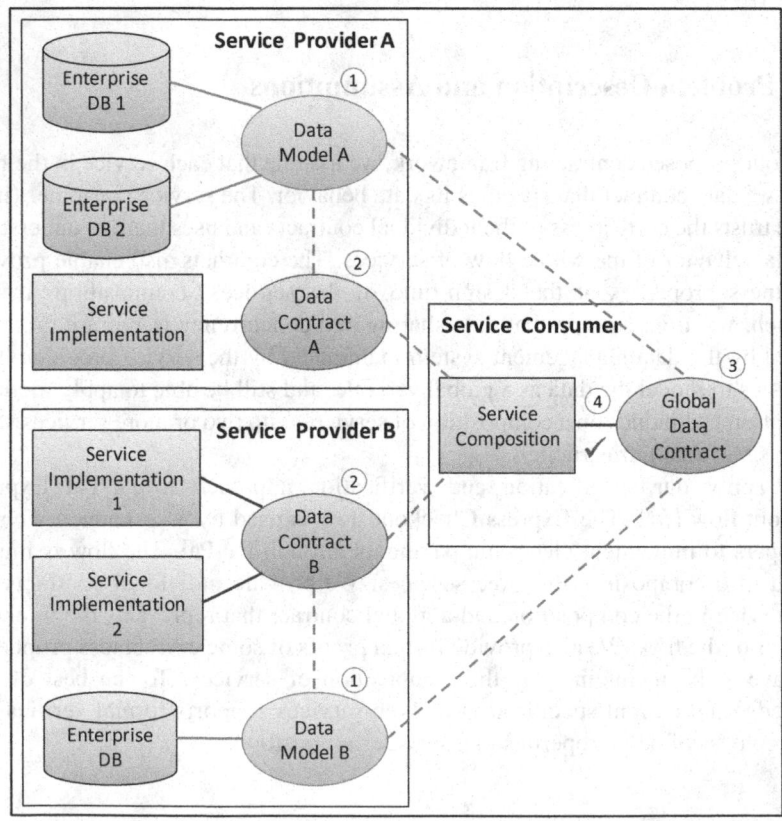

Fig. 5.1 Modeling and contracting framework for composite data-centric web services

ensure that any service implementation is correct with respect to the advertised service contract. Formal verification techniques are used to achieve this goal. Figure 5.1 shows that Service Provider B may choose between two different service implementations that are correct with respect to Data Contract B.

3. Assuming the correctness of individual service contracts, the service consumer can consult the individual contracts to understand the behavior of each service. The consumer then constructs a global data contract that reflects the consumer's intentions and the desired composition's side effects on the underlying data stores. The global data contract is written in terms of the individual data models.

4. The service consumer can formally verify the correctness of his or her composition with the global data contract. Automatic verification techniques may be used to facilitate this.

In the subsequent sections, we will demonstrate with an example of how we apply data modeling, contracting and verification of data-centric Web services according to the steps described above.

5.3 Case Study: PayPal's Express Checkout Flow

5.3.1 Problem Description and Assumptions

PayPal provides services for Express Checkout which makes it easier for customers to perform electronic payments through PayPal and allows sellers to accept PayPal payments while retaining control of the buyer and overall checkout flow. In this chapter, we apply our modeling and contracting framework to the PayPal Express Checkout flow. The flow is implemented by integrating three PayPal services: the *setExpressCheckout* service which initiates a payment transaction and returns a timestamped token. Upon success of the *setExpressCheckout* service call, the user is redirected to PayPal website to provide login credentials information. If the user approves the payment, PayPal redirects the user to a *success* URL, otherwise, PayPal redirects to the *cancel*URL. At the *success* URL, a call is made to the *getExpressCheckoutDetails* service to obtain information about the buyer from PayPal given the token previously generated by the *setExpressCheckout* service. Finally, a call to the *doExpressCheckout* service is used to complete the transaction by applying the payment and updating PayPal balances accordingly. Table 5.1 contains the description of these three services.

5.3.2 Data Modeling

For the purpose of specifying the PayPal flow composition, we use the generic class described earlier in Listing 4.1 to model the PayPal data store as given in Listing 5.1. The model is inferred based on online documentation and our own testing of the PayPal services.

Table 5.1 PayPal Express Checkout operations

Service	Description
SetExpressCheckout	Sets up the Express Checkout transaction. The service call must include the following information as input:
	• URL to the page on your website that PayPal redirects to after the buyer successfully logs into PayPal and approves the payment
	• URL to the page on your website that PayPal redirects to if the buyer cancels
	• Total amount of the order or your best estimate of the total. It should be as accurate as possible
GetExpressCheckoutDetails	Obtains information about the buyer from PayPal, including shipping information
DoExpressCheckoutPayment	Completes the Express Checkout transaction, including the actual total amount of the order

```
class PayPalDM

attribute transEntity: Set(TransRecord)

operation TransRecord findRecordByKey(key: String)
  ensures (result.token = key and result in this.transEntity)
       or result = Nil

operation Set(TransRecord) findRecordByCriteria(payerInfos: Set(PayerInfoType))
  ensures ∀rec in result, rec.payerInfo in payerInfos
       and result in this.transEntity

operation PayPalDM createRecord(rec: TransRecord)
   ensures result.transEntity = this.transEntity ∪ rec

operation PayPalDM deleteRecord(key: String)
  ensures result.transEntity = this.transEntity - this.findRecordByKey(key)

operation PayPalDM updateRecord(rec: TransRecord)
  requires findRecordByKey(rec.token) ≠ Nil
  ensures result.transEntity = deleteRecord(rec.token).createRecord(rec)

 end PayPalDM
```

```
class TransRecord

  attribute token: String //key
  attribute transAmount: Float
  attribute payerInfo: PayerInfoType
  attribute paymentStatus:{Processed, InProgress, Denied}

end TransRecord
```

Listing 5.1 The PayPal data model

We define the underlying Express Checkout record model, represented by the *TransRecord* class, as consisting of a token, a payment transaction amount *transAmount* and the corresponding payer information captured by the *payerInfo* attribute. A payment has a status represented by the *paymentStatus* attribute. The *token* attribute

```
String setExpressCheckout(Float sPaymentAmount, String successURL, String
cancelURL)
    modifies ppdm, rec, URL
    requires URL = checkoutURL
    ensures rec.token ≠ Nil and
            #ppdm.findRecordByKey(rec.token) = Nil
    ensures rec.payerInfo ≠ Nil and
            rec.transAmount = #sPaymentAmount and
            result = rec.token
    ensures (URL = successURL and rec.paymentStatus = InProgress) or
            (URL = cancelURL and rec.paymentStatus = Denied)
    ensures ppdm = #ppdm.createRecord(rec)


PayerInfoType getExpressCheckoutDetails(String gToken)
    modifies rec
    requires URL = successURL
    requires ppdm.findRecordByKey(gToken).payerInfo ≠ Nil
    ensures  rec = #ppdm.findRecordByKey(#gToken) and
             result = rec.payerInfo


boolean doExpressCheckout(String dToken, Float dPaymentAmount)
    modifies ppdm, rec
    requires URL = successURL
    requires ppdm.findRecordByKey(dToken).payerInfo ≠ Nil
    ensures rec = #ppdm.findRecordByKey(#dToken)
    ensures rec.transAmount =  #dPaymentAmount
    ensures (result = TRUE and rec.paymentStatus = Processed) or
            (result = FALSE and rec.paymentStatus = Denied)
    ensures ppdm = #ppdm.updateRecord(rec)
```

Listing 5.2 The individual data contracts of the PayPal Express Checkout services

is a timestamped token that is used by the three Express Checkout services to relate
different services calls to a one payment transaction. It is unique and hence we
choose to use it as the transaction record key. This example shows how our model
can reuse Web service data types defined in WSDL files; for example, we are reusing
PayerInfoType which is a complex data type used by different PayPal services to
hold the payer information such as name, shipping address, email and others. This
practice is very useful in minimizing the effort of modeling a service and ensuring
that the model complies with the original service design.

5.4   Data Contract

The data model is then used to annotate services with formal specifications represented as data contracts. Listing 5.2 shows how we use the PayPal model to expose
a data contract for each individual service in the PayPal flow. Our specification is
intended to be complete; i.e. any programming or state variable that is not explicitly
specified in the service contract is assumed to be unchanged after the service execution. We will use this assumption later in our proofs.

In Listing 5.2, we assume the variable *URL* to be a global string variable. The *URL* denotes the current Web page that is being accessed by the customer and whose code is being executed. As a demonstrative example, consider the contract of the *getExpressCheckoutDetails* service in Listing 5.2. The contract *requires* clauses specifies that the service should be invoked when two conditions are true; first, the *URL* variable should be equal to *successURL*. Second, the underlying data model should have a transaction record, identified by the service input *gToken*, and this record has a non-null payer information attribute. In other words, the service is called when a checkout transaction is set successfully and the payer information has been captured and saved in the data model. The contract's *ensures* clause specifies that the service returns the payer information related to that transaction record. The service does not change the data model since the contract does not explicitly defines a *modifies* clause.

In our specification of the PayPal services, we begin by defining a model variable *ppdm* of type *PayPalDM* representing the underlying data store. A model variable is a specification-only variable [62] that is used in conjunction with programming variables to model the state of the system. We include the model variable in each service specification to reflect the fact that all services are reading and updating the same data store and hence capturing dependency and compositional effect of services on that data store. Consequently, the state in our case is represented by service inputs and outputs in addition to the data store model variable. To simplify the specification, we also define a model variable *rec* of type *TransRecord* that is used to specify a transaction record, whenever needed.

5.5 Specification of Service Composition

We use formal specification to annotate the composition of services with a global data contract. The contract describes the intended behavior, from an integrator's point of view, for the flow of services based on the individual data contracts of each of the participating services. The flow implementation and the global contract are shown in Listing 5.3. We define global variables for both the data model variable and the URL as described before. We also assume a global variable *token* of type string. The *token* is the timestamped value, described before, that relates different service calls to the same transactions. Practically, global variables can be saved in a Web session.

Our implementation demonstrates the success case of calling *setExpressCheckout*. Whenever the e-commerce website customer is redirected by PayPal to the *successURL*, this implies that the user information is set successfully and linked to the current active express checkout transaction identified by the token value. We are not considering the implementation of the *cancelURL* page as it is application-specific and not handled by PayPal services. The global data contract shown in

```
PayerInfoType ExpressCheckoutFlow(Float paymentAmount, String successURL,
String cancelURL)

modifies ppdm, rec, URL, token
requires URL = checkoutURL;
ensures rec.transAmount = #paymentAmount and
        ppdm = #ppdm.createRecord(rec) and
        (result = rec.payerInfo and result ≠ Nil and
        rec.paymentStatus = Processed) or
        (result = Nil and rec.paymentStatus = Denied)
Begin
                                                              //state 0
  result := Nil;                                              //state 1
  token := setExpressCheckout(paymentAmount,successURL,cancelURL);  //state 2
  if (URL = successURL)                                       //state 3
    PayerInfoType payerInfo := getExpressCheckoutDetails(token);  //state 4
    boolean responseValue :=
      doExpressCheckout(token, payerInfo, paymentAmount);    //state 5
    if(responseValue)                                         //state 6
      result := payerInfo;                                    //state 7
    end if                                                    //state 8
  end if                                                      //state 9
End
```

Listing 5.3 The pseudocode of the PayPal Express Checkout composition

Listing 5.3 indicates that the flow should be called when *URL* is equal to the *checkoutURL*. The contract's *ensures* clauses specify the flow obligations as follows:

The flow creates a new transaction record with payment amount equal to the input payment amount. Also, the flow result is equal to the payer information associated with the newly created record in case the transaction is processed. Otherwise, the result is *Nil* and the payment transaction is marked as denied.

5.6 Proofs and Verification of Correctness

As depicted in Fig. 5.2, to prove that the implementation of the Express Checkout composed service is correct with respect to the specification, we must do two things:

1. Generate proof obligations for the composed service. Proof obligations—also called verification conditions—are a list of assertions that must be proved in order to verify correctness.
2. Discharge the proof obligations generated in (1), by proving each of the obligations using mathematical logic.

To generate the necessary proof obligations we use the symbolic reasoning technique introduced in [29]. Symbolic Reasoning can be seen as a generalization of code tracing, where object values are represented symbolically rather than concretely [63]. We begin by constructing a symbolic reasoning table. As described in Sect. 2.2.2, there are four columns in a symbolic reasoning table—the *state*, the

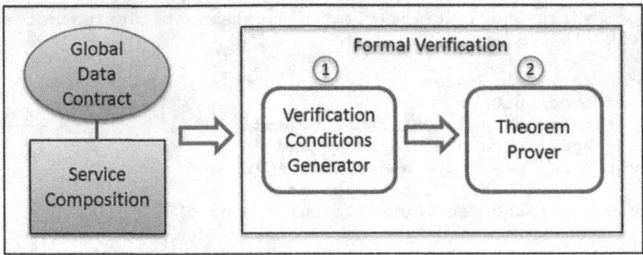

Fig. 5.2 The formal verification process

path condition, the *facts*, and the *obligations*. The *state* serves the same purpose as it does in the tracing table. The *path condition* column contains an assertion that must be true for a program to be in that particular state. The *facts* contain assertions that are true assuming that the state has been reached, and the *obligations* are assertions that need to be proved before a program can move to the next state. A detailed explanation of symbolic reasoning can be found in [63]. Table 5.2 is the symbolic reasoning table for the Express Checkout flow implementation. Variables are marked with the corresponding state. $ppdm_0$, for example, denotes the value of the data model variable *ppdm* at state 0.

We have added some implicit facts in Table 5.2 based on our assumption that the individual contracts are complete, as explained before. For example, the *getExpressCheckoutDetails* service does not specify explicitly any change to the *URL* variable and hence we can infer the fact that $URL_4 = URL_3$ as shown in state 4 in the reasoning table.

Next, we show how we can use the reasoning table to verify that the Express Checkout service is correct with respect to its data contract. The main idea is to prove that the obligations in the service contract are satisfied by the implementation. In order to accomplish that, we use facts from the symbolic table to prove obligations at the final state of the implementation. Following the natural reasoning technique in [63], an obligation at state k is proved by using facts at any state i, $0 \leq i \leq k$ that are consistent with the path condition of state k. As a demonstrative example, we will show the proof of the following obligation at state 9:

$$ppdm_9 = ppdm_0.createRecord(rec_9).$$

This obligation states that the PayPal database is updated by creating a new transaction record. We have three possible paths in the implementation in Listing 5.3; The first path spans states *1,2,3,4,5,6,7,8.a,9.a* in that order, the second path spans *1,2,3,4,5,6,7,8.b,9.a* and the third one spans *1,2,9.b*. We show here the proof for the first path as it is the most complex one and we leave the proofs of the other two cases for the reader. The proof goes as follows:

$$(1)\ ppdm_5 = ppdm_4.updateRecord(rec_5)$$

Table 5.2 The PayPal Express Checkout symbolic reasoning table

State	Path condition	Facts	Obligations
0		URL_0 = checkoutURL	
result := Nil;			
1		$result_1$ = Nil and URL_1 = URL_0 and $token_1$ = $token_0$ and $ppdm_1$ = $ppdm_0$ and rec_1 = rec_0	URL_1 = checkoutURL
token := setExpressCheckout(paymentAmount, successURL, cancelURL);			
2		rec_2.token ≠ Nil and $ppdm_0$.findRecordByKey(rec_2.token) = Nil and rec_2.payerInfo ≠ Nil and rec_2.transAmount = $paymentAmount_1$ and $token_2$ = rec_2.token and $ppdm_2$ = $ppdm_1$.createRecord(rec_2) (rec_2.paymentStatus = *InProgress* and URL_2 = successURL) or (rec_2.paymentStatus = *Denied* and URL_2 = cancelURL) and $result_2$ = $result_1$	
if (URL = successURL)			
3	URL_2 = successURL	URL_3 = URL_2 and $token_3$ = $token_2$ and $ppdm_3$ = $ppdm_2$ and rec_3 = rec_2 and $result_3$ = $result_2$	URL_3 = successURL and $ppdm_3$.findRecordByKey($token_3$).payerInfo ≠ Nil

(continued)

Table 5.2 (continued)

State	Path condition	Facts	Obligations
PayerInfoType payerInfo := getExpressCheckoutDetails(token);			
4	URL_2 = successURL	rec_4 = $ppdm_3$.findRecordByKey($token_3$) $payerInfo_4$ = rec_4.payerInfo and URL_4 = URL_3 and $token_4$ = $token_3$ and $ppdm_4$ = $ppdm_3$ and $result_4$ = $result_3$	URL_4 = successURL and $ppdm_4$. findRecordByKey($token_4$).payerInfo $\neq$ Nil
boolean responseValue := DoExpressCheckout(token, payerInfo, paymentAmount)			
5	URL_2 = successURL	rec_5 = $ppdm_4$.findRecordByKey($token_4$) rec_5.transAmount = $paymentAmount_4$ and $ppdm_5$ = $ppdm_4$.updateRecord(rec_5) and ($responseValue_5$ = TRUE and rec_5.paymentStatus = *Processed*) or($responseValue_5$ = FALSE and rec_5.paymentStatus = *Denied*) and URL_5 = URL_4 and $token_5$ = $token_4$ and $result_5$ = $result_4$	
if(responseValue)			
6	URL_2 = successURL and $responseValue_5$ = TRUE	URL_6 = URL_5 and $token_6$ = $token_5$ and $ppdm_6$ = $ppdm_5$ and rec_6 = rec_5 and $result_6$ = $result_5$	
result := payerInfo			
7	URL_2 = successURL and $responseValue_5$ = TRUE	URL_7 = URL_6 and $token_7$ = $token_6$ and $ppdm_7$ = $ppdm_6$ and rec_7 = rec_6 and $result_7$ = $payerInfo_6$	

end if		
8.a	$URL_2 = successURL$ and $responseValue_5 = TRUE$	$result_8 = result_7$ and $URL_8 = URL_7$ and $token_8 = token_7$ and $ppdm_8 = ppdm_7$ and $rec_8 = rec_7$
8.b	$URL_2 = successURL$ and $responseValue_5 = FALSE$	$result_8 = result_5$ and $URL_8 = URL_5$ and $token_8 = token_5$ and $ppdm_8 = ppdm_5$ and $rec_8 = rec_7$
end if		
9.a	$URL_2 = successURL$	$result_9 = result_8$ and $URL_9 = URL_8$ and $token_9 = token_8$ and $ppdm_9 = ppdm_8$ and $rec_9 = rec_8$	$rec_9.transAmount = paymentAmount_0$ and $ppdm_9 = ppdm_0.createRecord(rec_0)$ and $(result_9 = rec_9.payerInfo$ and $rec_9.paymentStatus = Processed)$or $(result_9 = Nil$ and $rec_9.paymentStatus = Denied)$
9.b	$URL_2 \neq successURL$	$result_9 = result_2$ and $URL_9 = URL_2$ and $token_9 = token_2$ and $ppdm_9 = ppdm_2$ and $rec_9 = rec_2$	

By referring to the specification of the *updateRecord* in Listing 6.2(b), this becomes:

(1') $ppdm_5 = ppdm_4.deleteRecord(rec_5.token).createRecord(rec_5)$

By facts at state 3 and 4 we know that $ppdm_4 = ppdm_3 = ppdm_2$, so this is equivalent to:

(1") $ppdm_5 = ppdm_2.deleteRecord(rec_5.token).createRecord(rec_5)$

From the facts at state 2, we know:

(2) $ppdm_2 = ppdm_1.createRecord(rec_2)$

Combining *(1")* and *(2)* gives us:

(3) $ppdm_5 = ppdm_1.createRecord(rec_2).deleteRecord(rec_5.token).createRecord(rec_5)$

From facts at states 2, 3, 4 and 5, we know that $rec_2.token = token_2$ *and* $token_5 = token_4 = token_3 = token_2$ and $rec_5 = ppdm_4.findRecordByKey(token_4)$, so *(3)* becomes:

(3') $ppdm_5 = ppdm_1.createRecord(rec_2).deleteRecord(token_2).createRecord(rec_5)$

By simplification, this becomes:

(3") $ppdm_5 = ppdm_1.createRecord(rec_5)$

By facts at state 9.a, 8.a, 7, 6 and 1, we know that $ppdm_9 = ppdm_8 = ppdm_7 = ppdm_6 = ppdm_5$ *and* $ppdm_1 = ppdm_0$ and $rec_9 = rec_8 = rec_7 = rec_6 = rec_5$ so this is equivalent to:

(3''') $ppdm_9 = ppdm_0.createRecord(rec_9)$

Similar proofs can be applied to other obligations listed in State 9 in the reasoning table.

5.7 Conclusions

It is worth noting here that, in the example above, none of the specified services modifies their input parameters. There is also no direct relationship between the services' inputs and outputs. For example, the *setExpressCheckout* service takes as input a set of URLs and a payment amount and it outputs a timestamped token. Hence, a contract that refers solely to the service inputs and outputs would fail to capture the side-effects of these services. In fact, each of these services applies many changes to the underlying data and there's indeed an indirect relationship between its inputs and outputs. There's no way however to fully specify these changes and relationships without referring to the data model variables. This is due to the fact that the main logic of these services lies in their interactions with the underlying database. Thus, comprehensive specifications of these interactions are indispensable for the understanding and correct invocation of these services by their consumers. The data specifications can be used to reason about specific data properties that must be maintained by a service composition. This is facilitated by our proposed model and data contracting framework.

From a practicality standpoint, the formal specification of a service remains largely a manual task. However, there have been efforts recently for integrating formal specification techniques into mainstream programming languages. The Java Modeling Language (JML) [64] for Java and the Spec# language [17] for C# are two examples. Both languages use constructs with similar syntax to the programming language that they specify. The advantage of using these languages in writing the contract is that it is easier for programmers to learn and less intimidating than languages that use special-purpose mathematical notations [64]. Both languages also support model variables, which enable the implementation of our framework where the data model is considered a specification-only variable as discussed earlier.

As for the verification of correctness, this process involves two steps as shown in Fig. 5.2. The first step includes the symbolic reasoning activity which is used to generate the contract obligations. This step is no more complex than compiling and hence it can be completely automated. The second step, which is proving the obligations from the available facts, can be automated for simple proofs. There has been an increased progress in this direction. For example, the authors of [65] present the RESOLVE verifying compiler that is used for both generating the obligations and proving simple ones. The compiler has been recently implemented as a Web tool [66]. The Boogie verifier [17] is another recent effort to provide an automatic verification tool for Spec# programs. The ESC/Java2 [67] is used to verify JML specifications for Java. For complex proofs, the verification task can be done in a semi-automatic way using computer-assisted theorem proving techniques. The Isabelle [68] interactive theorem prover is a major effort in this area and has been practically used to verify functional correctness of programs [69]. In Chap. 7, we implement the PayPal checkout flow using three of the state-of-the-art specification and verification tools to demonstrate the feasibility and study the limitations and practicality challenges.

Chapter 6
Specification and Verification of Transactional Web Service Composition

Abstract Web transactions are formed by integrating Web services in an ad-hoc manner. Distributed transaction protocols may be used to ensure that data integrity is maintained. However, these protocols require coordinated transaction management. Moreover, individual services must be transaction-aware in order to support necessary compensation operations whenever a transaction fails. These assumptions are unrealistic and impractical in the case of Web services that are generic by design and promote a loosely-coupled service integration practices.

In this chapter, we are exploring how our model can help verify data integrity properties based on the contract of individual services in an ad-hoc transaction. The goal is to show how the exposed contracts can help the services' integrator to design and plan their transactions while ensuring that their design preserves important data integrity conditions.

6.1 Background

Our proposed specification ad verification approach is based on the following assumptions:

- We consider transactional composition of Web service that adheres to the ACID properties (Atomicity, Consistency, Isolation, Durability).
- We consider short-lived transactions with pro-active service composition. A pro-active composition is an offline or pre-compiled composition of available services to form new services [70]. Services that compose in a pro-active manner are used at a very high rate over the Internet [71]. Developers build online applications by integrating services from different providers by consulting the services' WSDL specifications.
- Our proofs of correctness address both the atomicity and consistency aspects of an ACID transaction. Isolation and durability are assumed to be handled by the underlying data management infrastructure.
- We do not specify distributed concurrency. As described in [24], the formal specification of concurrent processes can be done using Petri Nets or axiomatic techniques that use temporal logic, which is beyond the scope of our specification methodology.

© Springer International Publishing Switzerland 2015   39
I. Saleh, *Formalizing Data-Centric Web Services*, Web-Scale Workflow
and Analytics, DOI 10.1007/978-3-319-24678-9_6

In order to achieve our goal, we specify a Web Service transaction. We begin by specifying some aspects of each service in order to verify some correctness properties at the transaction level. The specification is used to verify data integrity properties, mainly atomicity and consistency of the transaction, which should be maintained by the transaction implementation. Our approach is validated by an example where two sets of services from two different service providers are used to implement an e-commerce transaction. The scenario involves two different independent databases. In this setting, the global data integrity is no longer maintained by a database management system and hence it becomes the responsibility of the services integrators to maintain integrity within the transaction design. We show, using formal proofs, how our modeling and contracting framework can help verify data integrity conditions at design time.

6.2 Proposed Methodology

We are considering a "lightweight" specification case, meaning that we specify only aspects of the Web services that can be used to verify some implementation properties. In order to verify the integrity properties of a Web service transaction, we apply the following steps:

1. We define model variables representing the underlying data store for each of the participating providers.
2. We then specify a global data contract for the whole transaction of services. The contract describes the intended side-effects of the transaction on each of the underlying data stores. Mainly, the contract specifies obligations that guarantee the data integrity of the underlying data stores whether the transaction succeeds or fails.
3. Finally, we apply symbolic reasoning techniques described in Sect. 2.2.2 to verify that the transaction outcome satisfies important data integrity constraints as specified in the global contract.

6.3 Case Study: An E-Commerce Application Scenario

6.3.1 Problem Description and Assumptions

A developer feedback on a FedEx forum included the following question about Web services [12]:

> Hi, I need help with integrating FedEx with PayPal. I want to display FedEx shipping charges on the PayPal Order page. i.e. where the amount of the item is displayed, and charge the total sum (of the product amount and the shipping charges) from the customer. Can anybody suggest a site where PayPal and FedEx might have been integrated in such a way or where FedEx tools might have been used to calculate and charge shipping fees from the customer.

We consider the implementation of the proposed scenario where an e-commerce Website developer uses FedEx to ship orders to customers and uses PayPal to implement the electronic payment functionalities.

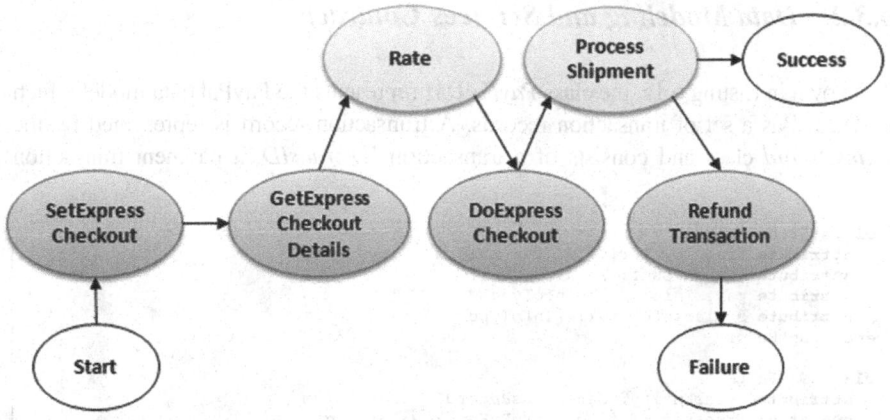

Fig. 6.1 E-commerce transaction integrating PayPal and FedEx Web services

The item purchase transaction is depicted in Fig. 6.1 and is described as follows:

1. The customer chooses to buy an item from the e-commerce Website.
2. The e-commerce Website invokes PayPal *SetExpressCheckout* service to initiate a payment transaction. The service is invoked with the item price plus an estimate of the shipping cost.
3. The Website redirects the customer to PayPal Website. The customer logins and reviews the shipping and billing information.
4. After customer confirmation, the PayPal Website redirects the customer back to the e-commerce Website.
5. The e-commerce Website invokes the *GetExpressCheckoutDetails* service to retrieve the customer's shipping and billing information.
6. The e-commerce Website invokes the FedEx *Rate* service to request a quote for the shipping of the item based on the exact shipping address.
7. The e-commerce Website displays for the customer the order total.
8. Upon the customer's confirmation, the e-commerce Website invokes the *DoExpressCheckout* service of PayPal with the exact order amount to actually charge the customer account with the order total.
9. The e-commerce Website then invokes the FedEx *ProcessShipment* service to initiate a FedEx shipment given the customer shipping address and the item details. The e-commerce Website is assumed to have a FedEx account that is used for payment.

The developer would like to consider this scenario as an ACID transaction and would like to ensure the "all-or-nothing" property. Consequently, if an error occurs in any of the steps above, a compensating action should be applied to undo any database update. For example, if the FedEx *ProcessShipment* service fails, the e-commerce Website should invoke the PayPal *RefundTransaction* service to compensate the customer's payment.

6.3.2   *Data Modeling and Services Contracts*

As shown in Listing 6.1a, the class *PayPalDM* represents the PayPal data model which is defined as a set of transaction records. A transaction record is represented by the *TransRecord* class and consists of a transaction ID *transID*, a payment transaction

```
class TransRecord
  attribute transID: String // The record's key
  attribute transAmount: float
  attribute payerInfo: PayerInfoType
  attribute sellerInfo: SellerInfoType
end TransRecord

class PayPalDM
  attribute transEntity: Set(TransRecord)
  operation TransRecord findRecordByKey(key: String)
    ensures (result.token = key  and result in this.transEntity)
            or result = Nil

operation Set(TransRecord)
   findRecordByCriteria(payerInfos: Set(PayerInfoType))
   ensures ∀rec in result, rec.payerInfo in payerInfos and
                           result in this.transEntity

operation PayPalDM createRecord(rec: TransRecord)
  ensures result.transEntity = this.transEntity ∪ rec

operation PayPalDM deleteRecord(key: String)
  ensures result.transEntity =
          this.transEntity - this.findRecordByKey(key)

operation PayPalDM updateRecord(rec: TransRecord)
  requires this.findRecordByKey(rec.transID) ≠ Nil
  ensures result.transEntity =
          this.deleteRecord(rec.transID).createRecord(rec)
end PayPalDM
```
(a) PayPal Data Model

```
String SetExpressCheckout(float sPaymentAmount,
          SellerInfoType seller, BuyerInfoType buyer)
modifies ppdm, pRec
ensures pRec.transID ≠ Nil and
        #ppdm.findRecordByKey(pRec.transID) = Nil and
        pRec.sellerInfo = #seller and
        pRec.payerInfo = #buyer and
        pRec.transAmount = #sPaymentAmount and
        result = pRec.transID and
        ppdm = #ppdm.createRecord(pRec)

PayerInfoType GetExpressCheckoutDetails(String gToken)
requires ppdm.findRecordByKey(gToken).payerInfo ≠ Nil
ensures  pRec = #ppdm.findRecordByKey(#gtoken) and
         result = pRec.payerInfo

void DoExpressCheckout(String dToken, float dPaymentAmount)

modifies ppdm
requires ppdm.findRecordByKey(dToken).payerInfo ≠ Nil
ensures #pRec = #ppdm.findRecordByKey(#dToken) and
        pRec.transAmount = #dPaymentAmount and
        pRec.payerInfo.balance =
        #pRec.payerInfo.balance - #dPaymentAmount and
        pRec.sellerInfo.balance =
        #pRec.sellerInfo.balance + #dPaymentAmount
ensures ppdm = #ppdm.updateRecord(pRec)
```

Listing 6.1 The formal specification of the FedEx services

```
void RefundTransaction(String transID)
modifies ppdm
requires ppdm.findRecordByKey(transID) ≠ Nil
ensures #pRec = #ppdm.findRecordByKey(#transID) and
        pRec.payerInfo.balance =
        #pRec.payerInfo.balance + #pRec.transAmount and
        pRec.sellerInfo.balance =
        #pRec.seller.balance - #pRec.transAmount and
         ppdm = #ppdm.updateRecord(pRec)
```

(b) Data Contracts of PayPal Services

```
class FedExRecord

   attribute trackingID: String //key
   attribute shipperAddress: Address
   attribute recipientAddress: Address
   attribute weight: float
   attribute packagingType: {BOX, ENVELOPE, YOUR_PACKAGING}
   attribute totalNetCharges: float

end FedExRecord

class FedExDM
   attribute shipmentEntity: Set(FedExRecord)
   // Similar definitions for findRecordByKey,
   // findRecordByCriteria, createRecord, deleteRecord
   // and updateRecord as in (a)
end FedExDM
```

(c) FedEx Data Model

```
float Rate(Address shipper, Address recipient,
           float weight, PackagingType packaging)

boolean ProcessShipment(Address shipper,
                        Address recipient,
                        float weight,
                        PackagingType packaging)
modifies fedm, fRec;
ensures if result = FALSE then
        fedm = #fedm and frec = #frec and
        if result = TRUE then
        fRec.trackingID ≠ Nil and
       #fedm.findRecordByKey(fRec.trackingID) = Nil and
        frec.shipperAddress = shipper and
        frec.recipientAddress = recipient and
        fRec.totalNetCharges =
        Rate(#shipper, #recipient, #weight, #packaging)
        and fedm = #fedm.createRecord(fRec)
```

(d) Data Contracts of FedEx Services

Listing 6.1 (continued)

amount *transAmount* and the corresponding payer and seller information captured by
the attributes *payerInfo* and *sellerInfo*, respectively. The *transID* attribute is a *timestamped* token that is used by the PayPal services to relate different services calls to a
one payment transaction. It is unique and hence we choose to use it as the transaction
record key.

Listing 6.1b shows how we use the proposed model to expose a data contract for each individual service in the PayPal flow. We consider four PayPal services: the *SetExpressCheckout* service, which initiates a payment transaction given the buyer and the seller information and returns a timestamped token. The *GetExpressCheckoutDetails* service is used obtain information about the buyer from PayPal given the token previously generated by a call to the *SetExpressCheckout* service. The *DoExpressCheckout* service is used to complete the transaction by applying the payment and updating PayPal balances accordingly. The *RefundTransaction*, as the name suggests, is called to refund a transaction identified by a token value.

Similarly, Listing 6.1c shows the data model for the FedEx data store. We define the FedEx record model, represented by the *FedExRecord* class, as consisting of a tracking ID, shipper and recipient information, package weight and type, and total shipment cost. The model supports similar data operations as in the *PayPalDM* class in Listing 6.1a. We have, however, omitted their definition in to avoid repetition. Listing 6.1d shows the specification of the FedEx services based on the proposed data model. We consider two FedEx services: The *Rate* service is used to provide pre-ship rating information given the shipper and the recipient addresses, and the item weight and packaging type. This service does not have to access the FedEx data store to calculate a rate and hence does not expose any data-related specification. The *ProcessShipment* service creates a FedEx shipment given the same information as the *Rate* service. The *ProcessShipment* has two possible return values; it either returns true when a shipment is created successfully, or it returns false on failure. For the sake of simplicity, we choose not to fully specify the failure conditions.

It should be noted that any programming or state variable that does not explicitly appears in the parameter list or in the *modifies* clause is assumed to be unchanged after the service execution. We will use this assumption later in our proofs.

6.3.3 Transaction Specification

The transaction is implemented as the composition of services described and specified in the previous section. The corresponding implementation is shown in Listing 6.2. For simplicity, the global contract shown only provides important obligations related to data integrity guarantees. The variable *returnValue* in Listing 7.6 denotes the transaction's output.

We investigate how the data contract of individual services can be used to verify integrity properties including:

– On successful completion of the transaction, the customer's PayPal account is charged exactly the item cost plus the shipping cost.
– On successful completion of the transaction, the e-commerce FedEx account is only charged the item shipping cost.
– On transaction failure, the customer's PayPal account remains intact.

```
boolean CheckoutTransaction(Item item,
                            SellerInfoType seller,
                            BuyerInfoType buyer)
modifies ppDm, feDm
ensures if result = TRUE then
      seller.balance = #seller.balance + #item.price
                     + Rate(#seller.address,
                            #buyer.address,
                            #item.weight,
                            PackagingType.YOUR_PACKAGING) and
      buyer.balance = #buyer.balance - #item.price
                     - Rate(#seller.address,
                            #buyer.address,
                            #item.weight,
                            PackagingType.YOUR_PACKAGING)
      if result = FALSE then
         seller.balance = #seller.balance and
         buyer.balance = #buyer.balance
BEGIN
returnValue := FALSE;
String token := SetExpressCheckout(item.price, seller, buyer);
PayerInfoType payerInfo := GetExpressCheckoutDetails(token);
float totalCharge:= Rate(seller.Address,
                         payerInfo.Address, item.weight,
                         YOUR_PACKAGING);
DoExpressCheckout(token, totalCharge + item.price);
if ProcessShipment(seller.Address,
                   payerInfo.Address,
                   item.weight,
                   YOUR_PACKAGING) then
      returnValue := TRUE;
else
      RefundTransaction(token);
end if
END
```

Listing 6.2 The pseudo-code of the item checkout transaction

- On transaction failure, no shipment is created on FedEx.
- Whenever the e-commerce FedEx account is charged for a shipping cost, the customer PayPal account is charged with the same cost.

6.3.4   Verification of Data Integrity Properties

In this section, we show how service specifications facilitate verification of data correctness properties in a composition of services. We first show a tracing table (Table 6.1) where we are interested in verifying the updates in the seller and buyer balances after the transaction terminates. A correct transaction implementation must ensure that both balances are updated consistently on transaction success, or left intact on transaction failure. In Table 6.1, we are tracing the case where PayPal services are successfully executed, while the FedEx ProcessShipment service fails. In this case, a correct transaction design would leave the seller and buyer balances intact since the item shipment failed. In the tracing table below, a double question mark (??) for a value indicates that the variable's value is unspecified. Values that are changed in a

Table 6.1 The tracing table of the Item Checkout transaction

State	Facts
0	
	item = [price = 10.0,…] and buyer = [Name = "MyBuyer", balance = 100.0,…] and seller = [Name = "MySeller", balance = 500.0, …] and ppdm = [transEntity = {??}] fedm = [shipmentEntity = {??}]
result := FALSE	
1	result = FALSE No change in ppdm and fedm
String token := SetExpressCheckout(item.price, seller, buyer);	
2	token = ?? ppdm = [transEntity = {??,[transID=token, payerInfo =[Name = "MyBuyer", balance = 100.0,…], sellerInfo =[Name = "MySeller", balance = 500.0, …], transAmount = 10.0]}] *No change in fedm*
PayerInfoType payerInfo := GetExpressCheckoutDetails(token);	
3	payerInfo =[Name = "MyBuyer", balance = 100.0,…] *No change in ppdm and fedm*
float totalCharge:= Rate(payerInfo.Address, seller.Address, item.weight, PackagingType.YOUR_PACKAGING);	
4	totalCharge =5.0 No change in ppdm and fedm
DoExpressCheckout(token, totalCharge + item.price);	
5	ppdm = [transEntity = {??,[transID=token, payerInfo =[Name = "MyBuyer", balance = 85.0,…], sellerInfo =[Name = "MySeller", balance = 515.0, …], transAmount = 15.0]}] *No change in fedm*
if(ProcessShipment(seller.Address, buyer.Address, item.weight, PackagingType.YOUR_PACKAGING)) then	
6	Assuming the service fails and returns FALSE: No change in ppdm and fedm
RefundTransaction(token);	
7	ppdm = [transEntity = {??,[transID=token, payerInfo =[Name = "MyBuyer", balance = 100.0,…], sellerInfo =[Name = "MySeller", balance = 500.0, …], transAmount = 15.0]}] No change in fedm

given state are marked in bold. We are mainly interested in tracing changes in the PayPal and FedEx data models represented by the model variables ppdm and fedm, respectively. We assume a starting state specified by the values of the variables in state 0. We also assume that the item shipping cost is $5.0.

As can be seen from the tracing table, the transaction terminates with the following state for the data models:

```
ppdm = [transEntity = {??,[transID=token,
       payerInfo =[Name = "MyBuyer", balance = 100.0,…],
       sellerInfo =[Name = "MySeller", balance= 500.0,…],
       transAmount=15.0]}] and
fedm = [shipmentEntity = {??}]
```

These assertions indicate that a new transaction record is created in the PayPal data model while the buyer and seller balances do not change from their initial values (100.0 and 500.0, respectively). The FedEx model remains unchanged; no new shipment is created. This outcome is consistent with the correct transaction behavior expected by the transaction's developer in the case of the shipment failure. Similar tracing tables can be constructed to verify the transaction correctness under different run-time assumptions.

It should be noted that tracing through the transaction logic as shown in Table 6.1 would not be possible if services only expose their syntax interfaces as it is the case in current Web service specification standards such as the WSDL. This is however possible using our proposed contracting framework since they enable the services' consumer to reason about a service output and its data side-effects.

Alternatively, a transaction developer can use symbolic reasoning technique, introduced in [29], as a way to generate the proof obligations required in formal verification. Symbolic reasoning can be seen as a generalization of code tracing, where object values are represented symbolically rather than concretely. A detailed explanation of symbolic reasoning can be found in [63] along with a demonstrative example. There are four columns in a symbolic reasoning table—the state, the path condition, the facts, and the obligations. The state serves the same purpose as it does in the tracing table. The path condition column contains an assertion that must be true for a program to be in that particular state. The facts contain assertions that are true assuming that the state has been reached, and the obligations are assertions that need to be proved before a program can move to the next state.

Table 6.2 is the symbolic reasoning table for the item Checkout transaction. Variables are marked with the corresponding state. For example, $ppdm_1$ denotes the value of the PayPal data model variable $ppdm$ at state 1. Next, we show how we can use the reasoning table to formally verify that the item checkout transaction preserves data consistency between the FedEx and PayPal databases by ensuring the all-or-nothing property. The main idea is to prove that the obligations in the service contract are satisfied by the implementation. In order to accomplish that, we use facts from the symbolic table to prove obligations at the final state of the implementation. Following the natural reasoning technique in [63], an obligation at state k is proved by using facts at any state i, $0 \leq i \leq k$ that are consistent with the path condition of state k.

Table 6.2 The symbolic reasoning table of the Item Checkout transaction

State	Path condition	Facts	Obligations
0			
		returnValue := FALSE	
1		$returnValue_1$ = FALSE and $pRec_1$ = $pRec_0$ and $fRec_1$ = $fRec_0$ and $ppdm_1$ = $ppdm_0$ and $fedm_1$ = $fedm_0$ $seller_1$ = $seller_0$ and $buyer_1$ = $buyer_0$	
		String token := SetExpressCheckout(item.price, seller, buyer);	
2		$pRec_2.transID \neq Nil$ and $ppdm_2.findRecordByKey(pRec_2.transID)$ = Nil and $pRec_2.payerInfo$ = $buyer_1$ and $pRec_2.sellerInfo$ = $seller_1$ and $pRec_2.transAmount$ = $item_1.price$ and $token_2$ = $pRec_2.transID$ and $ppdm_2$ = $ppdm_1.createRecord(pRec_2)$ and $fRec_2$ = $fRec_1$ and $fedm_2$ = $fedm_1$ and $returnValue_2$ = FALSE	$ppdm_2.findRecordByKey(token_2)$ $.payerInfo \neq Nil$
		PayerInfoType payerInfo := GetExpressCheckoutDetails(token);	
3		$pRec_3$ = $ppdm_2.findRecordByKey(token_2)$ and $payerInfo_3$ = $pRec_3.payerInfo$ and $fRec_3$ = $fRec_2$ and $ppdm_3$ = $ppdm_2$ and $fedm_3$ = $fedm_2$ and $returnValue_3$ = FALSE and $token_3$ = $token_2$	
		float totalCharge := Rate(payerInfo.Address, seller.Address, item.weight, PackagingType.YOUR_PACKAGING);	

4	$payerInfo_4 = payerInfo_3$ and $pRec_4 = pRec_3$ and $fRec_4 = fRec_3$ and $ppdm_4 = ppdm_3$ and $fedm_4 = fedm_3$ and $returnValue_4 = FALSE$ and $token_4 = token_3$	$ppdm_4.findRecordByKey(token_4).$ $payerInfo \neq Nil$

DoExpressCheckout(token, totalCharge + item.price);

5		$pRec_4 = ppdm_4.findRecordByKey(token_4)$ and $pRec_5.transID = pRec_4.transID$ and $pRec_5.transAmount = totalCharge_4 + item_4.price$ and $pRec_5.payerInfo.balance = pRec_4.payerInfo.balance - totalCharge_4 - item_4.price$ and $pRec_5.sellerInfo.balance = pRec_4.sellerInfo.balance + totalCharge_4 + item_4.price$ and $ppdm_5 = ppdm_4.updateRecord(pRec_5)$ and $fRec_5 = fRec_4$ and $fedm_5 = fedm_4$ and $returnValue_5 = FALSE$ and $token_5 = token_4$

if(ProcessShipment(seller.Address, payerInfo.Address, item.weight, YOUR_PACKAGING)) then

6	$result_6 = TRUE$	$fRec_6.trackingID \neq Nil$ and $fRec_6.totalNetCharges = Rate(seller_5.Address, payerInfo_5.Address, item_5.weight, YOUR\_PACKAGING)$ and $fedm_6 = fedm_5.createRecord(fRec_6)$ and $pRec_6 = pRec_5$ and $ppdm_6 = ppdm_5$ and $returnValue_6 = FALSE$ and $token_6 = token_5$

(continued)

Table 6.2 (continued)

State	Path condition	Facts	Obligations
returnValue := TRUE;			
7	$result_6 =$ TRUE	$pRec_7 = pRec_6$ and $fRec_7 = fRec_6$ and $ppdm_7 = ppdm_6$ and $fedm_7 = fedm_6$ and $returnValue_7 =$ TRUE and $token_7 = token_6$	
else			
8	$result_6 =$ FALSE	$pRec_8 = pRec_5$ and $fRec_8 = fRec_5$ and $ppdm_8 = ppdm_5$ and $fedm_8 = fedm_5$ and $returnValue_8 =$ FALSE and $token_8 = token_5$	$ppdm_8.findRecordByKey(token_8) \neq$ Nil
RefundTransaction(token);			
9	$result_6 =$ FALSE	$pRec_8 = ppdm_8.findRecordByKey(token_8)$ and $pRec_9.transID = pRec_8.transID$ and $pRec_9.transAmount = pRec_8.transAmount$ and $pRec_9.payerInfo.balance = pRec_8.payerInfo.balance + pRec_8.transAmount$ and $pRec_9.sellerInfo.balance = pRec_8.sellerInfo.balance - pRec_8.transAmount$ and $ppdm_9 = ppdm_8.updateRecord(pRec_9)$ and $fRec_9 = fRec_8$ and $fedm_9 = fedm_8$ and $returnValue_9 =$ FALSE and $token_9 = token_8$	

end if		
10.a	$result_6$ = TRUE	$pRec_{10}$ = $pRec_7$ and $fRec_{10}$ = $fRec_7$ and $ppdm_{10}$ = $ppdm_7$ and $fedm_{10}$ = $fedm_7$ and $returnValue_8$ = TRUE and $token_{10}$ = $token_7$	if $returnValue_{10}$ = TRUE then $seller_{10}$.balance = $seller_0$.balance + $item_0$.price + Rate($seller_0$.address, $buyer_0$.address, $item_0$.weight, YOUR_PACKAGING) and $buyer_{10}$.balance = $buyer_0$.balance - $item_0$.price - Rate($seller_0$.address, $buyer_0$.address, $item_0$.weight, YOUR_PACKAGING) if $returnValue_{10}$ = FALSE then $seller_{10}$.balance = $seller_0$.balance and $buyer_{10}$.balance = $buyer_0$.balance
10.b	$result_6$ = FALSE	$pRec_{10}$ = $pRec_9$ and $fRec_{10}$ = $fRec_9$ and $ppdm_{10}$ = $ppdm_9$ and $fedm_{10}$ = $fedm_9$ and $returnValue_8$ = FALSE and $token_{10}$ = $token_9$	

As a demonstrative example, we will show the proof of the following obligation at state 10:

```
if returnValue₁₀ = FALSE then
seller₁₀.balance = seller₀.balance and
buyer₁₀.balance = buyer₀.balance
```

This obligation states that if the transaction returns a false value, neither the seller or buyer balances are updated. As seen from the symbolic reasoning table, the transaction terminates in state 10.a if the value returned from ProcessShipment (and hence, returnValue10) is true, or in state 10.b if it is false. Consequently, the above-mentioned obligation that we are proving relies on the facts in state 10.b. The proof of the obligation goes as follows:

From Facts at state 1:

```
(1) ppdm₁ = ppdm₀ and seller₁ = seller₀ and buyer₁ = buyer₀
```

From Facts at state 2:

```
(2) ppdm₂ = ppdm₁.createRecord(pRec₂) and
    pRec₂ = [transID = token₂,
            payerInfo = buyer₁,
            sellerInfo = seller₁,
            transAmount = item₁.price]
```

Combining (1) and (2) gives us:

```
(3)  ppdm₂ = ppdm₀.createRecord(pRec₂) and
     pRec₂ = [transID = token₂,
            payerInfo = buyer₀,
            sellerInfo = seller₀,
            transAmount = item₁.price]
```

By facts at state 3 and 4 we know that

```
ppdm₄ = ppdm₃ = ppdm₂ and pRec₄ = pRec₃ and
pRec₃ = ppdm₂.findRecordByKey(token₂) which is equal to pRec₂, so (3)
becomes:
(3') ppdm₄ = ppdm₀.createRecord(pRec₄) and
     pRec₄ = [transID = token₂,
            payerInfo = buyer₀,
            sellerInfo = seller₀,
            transAmount = item₁.price]
```

From facts at state 5:

```
pRec₄ = ppdm₄.findRecordByKey(token₄)
```

From the specification of *findRecordByKey* in Listing 7.3, this implies that:

```
(4) pRec₄.transID = token₄
```

Also, at state 5, we know that:

```
(5) pRec₅.transID = pRec₄.transID and pRec₅.transAmount = total-
Charge₄ + item₄.price and
pRec₅.payerInfo.balance = pRec₄.payerInfo.balance
                          - totalCharge₄
                          - item₄.price and
pRec₅.sellerInfo.balance= pRec₄.sellerInfo.balance
                          + totalCharge₄
                          + item₄.price and
```

Combining (3'), (4) and (5) gives us the specification of $pRec_5$:

```
(6) pRec₅ = [transID = token₄,
             payerInfo = buyer₅,
             sellerInfo = seller₅,
             transAmount = totalCharge₄
                           + item₄.price]
```

Where,

```
seller₅.balance = seller₀.balance
                  + totalCharge₄
                  + item₄.price and
buyer₅.balance = buyer₀.balance
                 - totalCharge₄
                 - item₄.price
```

We know from facts at state 8 that $ppdm_8 = ppdm_5$ and $pRec_8 = pRec_5$, so this gives us:

```
(7) pRec₈ = [transID = token₄,
             payerInfo = buyer₈,
             sellerInfo = seller₈,
             transAmount = totalCharge₄ + item₄.price]
```

Where,

```
seller₈.balance = seller₀.balance
                + totalCharge₄
                + item₄.price and
buyer₈.balance = buyer₀.balance
                - totalCharge₄
                - item₄.price
```

From facts at state 9,

```
ppdm₉ = ppdm₈.updateRecord(pRec₉) and
pRec₉ = [transID = token₈,
 payerInfo = buyer₉,
 sellerInfo = seller₉,
 transAmount = transAmount₈]
```

Where,

```
seller₉.balance = seller₈.balance - pRec₈.transAmount and
buyer₉.balance = buyer₈.balance + pRec₈.transAmount
```

Substituting from (7):

```
(8) seller₉.balance = seller₀.balance
                    + totalCharge₄
                    + item₄.price
                    - totalCharge₄
                    - item₄.price   and
    buyer₉.balance = buyer₀.balance
                    - totalCharge₄
                    - item₄.price
                    + totalCharge₄
                    + item₄.price
```

By simplification, this becomes:

```
(8') seller₉.balance = seller₀.balance and
    buyer₉.balance = buyer₀.balance
```

From facts at state 10.b:

```
pRec₁₀ = pRec₉ and ppdm₁₀ = ppdm₉, Then (8) becomes:
(8") seller₁₀.balance = seller₀.balance and
    buyer₁₀.balance = buyer₀.balance
```

Similar proofs can be applied to other obligations in the reasoning table. These formal proofs provide a verification of important correctness properties that a transaction design needs to maintain after its execution.

6.4   Conclusions

In this chapter, we show how that the formal methods can facilitate the specification and verification of transactional Web service composition. We demonstrate by using a real-life example how formal methods can be useful in providing data integrity guarantees within a Web transaction. We hence provide Web service consumers with valuable tools and guidelines that enable verifying correctness of their Web service-based applications. Our approach has a sound formal foundation which opens the opportunities of many automated applications that exploit the exposed specification in order to deduce facts about service behavior.

Chapter 7
Model Implementation

Abstract In this chapter, we show an implementation of our model and a case study using three of the state-of-the-art specification languages, namely JML [72], Dafny [73] and RESOLVE [65]. Our goal is to show the feasibility of our model implementation and to study the current challenges and limitations of formal languages and verification tools. Our experiment described here show that, despite the limitations of the tools, we could still reason about a service-based implementation and obtain some proofs of correctness.

We are using a simplified version of the PayPal checkout flow, described in Chap. 5, as a composition case study that we formally model and specify using the proposed framework.

7.1 The Specification Language

In order to implement the proposed model using a specification language, the language design must support the following constructs:

- Specification-only variables (a.k.a *ghost* variables)

- The data model in our framework is defined as a specification-only variable that is used to represent the underlying database and specifying the service-to-data interactions.
- Side-effect free methods
- These are used to define the basic data operations supported by the data model as defined in Chap. 5. These operations are used in the specification of a service interface.
- Specification of interface-only methods

- Web services are used based on their exposed APIs. Programmers depend on the APIs signatures in order to call services within their code. A specification language used to specify Web services must hence support a mechanism to specify interface-only methods. A verifier in this case can be used to ensure the consistency of the specification and not to prove its correctness.

© Springer International Publishing Switzerland 2015

I. Saleh, *Formalizing Data-Centric Web Services*, Web-Scale Workflow and Analytics, DOI 10.1007/978-3-319-24678-9_7

7.2   Implementation Modules

Based on the model discussed earlier, the specification and verification of the PayPal Express Checkout flow entails the implementation the three modules shown below in Fig. 7.1:

– Module (1): The PayPal data model.
– Module (2): The data contract for each of the three PayPal services.
– Module (3): The implementation and the data contract of the PayPal Express Checkout that composes the three PayPal services.

   In the following sections, we discuss parts of the implementation of these three modules using the Dafny, JML and RESOLVE languages.

7.3   Dafny

7.3.1   The Language Design

Dafny [73] is a class-based specification language. A Dafny class can declare variables, methods, and functions. The language supports specification-only variables through ghost variables. It also supports user-defined mathematical functions that

Fig. 7.1 The implementation modules

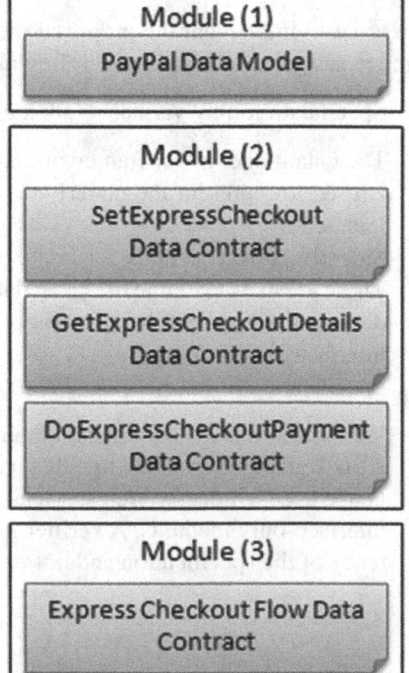

can be used in writing specifications. The language has a verifier that translates it to the Boogie intermediate verification language [74]. A Boogie tool is then used to generate first-order verification conditions that are passed to the Z3 theorem prover [75]. The types supported by Dafny are booleans, mathematical integers, references to instances of user-defined generic classes, sets, sequences, and user-defined algebraic datatypes. Specifications in Dafny include standard pre- and postconditions, framing constructs, and termination metrics.

7.3.2 Implementation Details

7.3.2.1 Module (1): The Data Model

Listing 7.1 is an excerpt of the model implementation in Dafny. The implementation includes a definition of the *TransRecord* class. Due to the abstraction level of the Dafny language, we have simplified the model in terms of the data types used; sequences of integers for example are used to represent strings. Sequences are also used to represent the collection of record representing the *transEntity* attribute in the model class. The *transEntity* attribute is defined as a *ghost* variable as it is declared

```
1  class TransRecord {
2    var token: seq<int>; //seq<int> is used to represent a string
3    var transAmount: int;
4    var payerInfo: seq<int>;
5    var paymentStatus: seq<int>;
6  }//end of class TransRecord
7
8  class PayPalDM{
9  // The model uses a 'sequence' to define the collection of records
10 ghost var transEntity: seq<TransRecord>;
11
12 function isValid(): bool
13 reads *;
14 {
15   (0 <=|transEntity|) &&
16   (forall j :: j >= 0 && j < |transEntity| ==> transEntity[j] != null)
17 }
18
19 function findRecordByKey(key: seq<int>, i: int):  TransRecord
20 requires isValid();
21 requires i >= 0 && i <= |transEntity|;
22 reads *;
23 decreases |transEntity|-i; //specifies that the recursion terminates
24   {
25   if i >= |transEntity| then null
26   else if transEntity[i].token == key then transEntity[i]
27         else findRecordByKey(key, i+1)
28 }
    ...
88 }//end of class PayPalDM
89
```

Listing 7.1 An excerpt of the data model implementation in Dafny

for specification-only purposes. For the same reason, the methods supported by the model are defined using Dafny's mathematical functions. In Dafny, mathematical functions are declarative, side-effect free functions that can be used to write specifications. The domain of a function is defined by a *requires* clause. The *reads* clause gives a frame for the function, saying which objects the function may depend on. The *decreases* clause gives a termination and the function's body defines the value of the function [73]. We hence implemented a body for each function in the data model to define its value.

Dafny does not support the definition of object invariants. Instead, validity functions are used, e.g. the *isValid()* function in the model implementation specifies the conditions for a valid object. A method that reserves the object validity must reference the validity function in its pre and post conditions. In our example, the validity of a data model implies that the collection of records has a zero or more records and that each record in the collection is not a null object.

7.3.2.2 Module (2): Individual Service Contracts

Listing 7.2 is the Dafny specification of one of the PayPal service, namely the *SetExpressCheckout*. The implementation defines two ghost variables; *ppdm* representing the PayPal data model and *rec* representing a record in the PayPal data model which is used to specify records created or updated by any of the specified services. The specified method represents a service API and hence no implementation is provided.

```
90 class ExpressCheckoutAPI{
91
92 ghost var ppdm: PayPalDM;
93 ghost var rec: TransRecord;

    ...

129 method setExpressCheckout(sPaymentAmount: int) returns (sToken: seq<int>)
130 modifies ppdm, rec;
131 requires isValid();
132 ensures isValid();
133 //The following 'ensures' is redundant but prevents a verifier's error at
    line 135 ('possible violation of function precondition')
134 ensures old(ppdm).isValid();
135 ensures old(ppdm).findRecordByKey(sToken, 0) == null;
136 ensures ppdm.findRecordByKey(sToken, 0) != null;
137 ensures sToken == rec.token;
138 //73 is the code for 'i' which is abbreviation for 'in progress'
139 ensures ppdm.transEntity == old(ppdm).createRecord(rec) && rec != null &&
140 rec.transAmount == sPaymentAmount && rec.paymentStatus == [73] &&
141 rec.payerInfo != [];
142 ensures ppdm.findRecordByKey(sToken, 0).payerInfo != [];
143 {
144 }
```

Listing 7.2 The Specification of the *SetExpressCheckout* PayPal Service in Dafny

As seen in the code snippet, some redundant assertions are added to the service specification to avoid verification errors. For example, the validity of the *ppdm* object before method invocation is specified using the *requires* clause at line 131. While the validity of *old(ppdm)* can be inferred from this *requires* clause, the Boogie verifier fails to prove it and hence generate error signaling the violation of *findRecordBykey* precondition. The redundant *ensures* clause at line 134 is added to eliminate the verifier error.

7.3.2.3 Module (3): The Global Contract

Listing 7.3 is the implementation of the PayPal Express Checkout flow along with its data contract using the Dafny language. The flow returns the payer information on success and an empty string on failure. Again, some redundant assertions are added into the contract to compensate for some of the verifier limitations.

7.3.3 Verification Results

Table 7.1 summarizes the verification results obtained by applying the Boogie verifier to the Dafny code. As can be seen in the table, the verifier fails to prove the postconditions of the three PayPal services since their implementations are not

```
90 class ExpressCheckoutAPI{
91
92 ghost var ppdm: PayPalDM;
93 ghost var rec: TransRecord;
...
102 method expressCheckoutFlow(paymentAmount: int) returns (flowResult: seq<int>)
103 modifies ppdm, rec;
104 requires isValid();
105 //The following 'ensures' is redundant but prevents a verifier's error at line 108
106 //('possible violation of function precondition')
107 ensures old(ppdm).isValid();
108 ensures old(ppdm).findRecordByKey(rec.token, 0) == null;
109 ensures rec.transAmount == old(paymentAmount) &&
110        ppdm.transEntity == old(ppdm).createRecord(rec);
111 //80 is the code for 'p' which is used as abbreviation for 'processed'
112 ensures flowResult!=[]==>flowResult== ppdm.findRecordByKey(rec.token, 0).payerInfo
113        && ppdm.findRecordByKey(rec.token, 0).paymentStatus == [80];
114 //68 is the code for 'd' which is used as abbreviation for 'denied'
115 ensures flowResult==[]==> ppdm.findRecordByKey(rec.token,0).paymentStatus == [68];
116 {
117   var token: seq<int>;
118   var payerInfo: seq<int>;
119   var responseValue: bool;
120   flowResult := [];
121   call token := setExpressCheckout(paymentAmount);
122   call payerInfo := getExpressCheckoutDetails(token);
123   call responseValue := doExpressCheckout(token, paymentAmount);
124   if (responseValue == true) {
125      flowResult := payerInfo;
126   }
127   return;
128 }
...
178      } // end of class ExpressCheckoutAPI
```

Listing 7.3 The Dafny implementation and specification of the PayPal Express Checkout flow

Table 7.1 Verification results using the Boogie verifier

Method/function	Verification time (s)	Verification result
Class PayPalAPI		
isValid	0.0240015	Passed successfully
expressCheckoutFlow	0.1720099	Passed successfully
setExpressCheckout	0.0810046	Postconditions cannot be verified
getExpressCheckoutDetails	0.0570033	Postconditions cannot be verified
doExpressCheckout	0.089005	Postconditions cannot be verified
Class DataModel		
isValid	0.0120008	Passed successfully
findRecordByKey	0.0220012	Passed successfully
findRecordByCriteria	0.0300017	Passed successfully
findRecordIndex	0.0200012	Passed successfully
deleteRecord	0.0350019	Passed successfully
createRecord	0.0120007	Passed successfully
updateRecord	0.0220013	Passed successfully
Program Interpretation	1.8731069	
Total	2.44914	

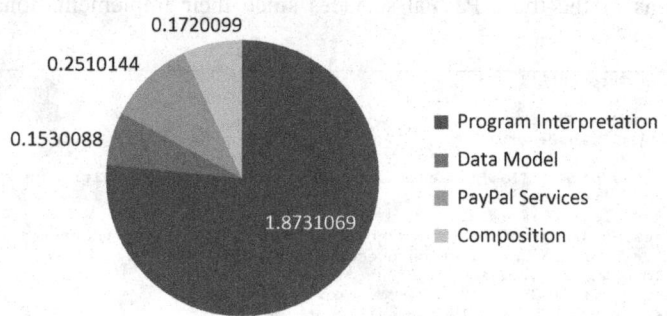

Fig. 7.2 The distribution of the verification time using the Boogie verifier

provided. This can be however safely ignored since modular verification can still be applied to the service composition.

Figure 7.2 depicts the distribution of the time among the different verification tasks.

7.4   The Java Modeling Language

7.4.1   The Language Design

The Java Modeling Language (JML) is a specification language that is used to specify Java modules. JML annotations are appended to Java code as comments proceeded by the at-sign (@). JML uses a *requires* clause to specify a method's pre-conditions and an *ensures* clause to specify the post-conditions. The \result variable denotes the output of a method. The \old prefix denotes the value of a variable before the method invocation. A complete reference of the JML syntax can be found in [76].

7.4.2   Implementation Details

7.4.2.1   Module (1): The Data Model

Listing 7.4 is the data model implementation in JML (we have omitted the definition of the *TransRecord* class to avoid repetition). An array is used to represent the collection of record representing the *transEntity* attribute in the model class. Similar to Dafny, the *transEntity* attribute is defined as a *ghost* variable as it is declared for

```
1  abstract class PayPalDM {
2
3  //@ public ghost TransRecord[] transEntity;
4
5  //@ ensures (\exists int j; j > 0 &&
6              j < transEntity.length; transEntity[j].myEquals(\result) )
7              || (\result == null);
8  public /*@ pure @*/abstract TransRecord findRecordByKey(/*@ non_null*/ String
   key);
9
10 //@ ensures (\forall int i; i > 0 && i < \result.length;
11             (\exists int j; j > 0 && j < payerInfos.length;
12               \result[i].payerInfo == payerInfos[j] ));
13 public /*@ pure @*/abstract TransRecord[] findRecordByCriteria(/*@ non_null */
14                                             String[] payerInfos);
15
16 //@ ensures (\exists int j; j > 0 &&
17             j < transEntity.length; transEntity[j].myEquals(rec));
18 //@ ensures findRecordByKey(rec.token) != null;
19 public /*@ pure @*/ abstract PayPalDM createRecord(/*@ non_null*/ Record rec);
20
21 //@ ensures (\forall int j; j > 0 && j < transEntity.length;
22              transEntity[j].token != key);
23 //@ ensures findRecordByKey(\old(key)) == null;
24 public /*@ pure @*/ abstract PayPalDM deleteRecord(/*@ non_null*/String key);
25
26 //@ requires findRecordByKey(rec.token) != null;
27 //@ ensures \result == this.deleteRecord(rec.token).createRecord(rec);
28 public /*@ pure @*/ abstract PayPalDM updateRecord(/*@ non_null*/ TransRecord
   rec);
29
30 }
```

Listing 7.4 The implementation and specification of the data model in JML

specification-only purposes. The methods supported by the model are defined as abstract *pure* methods. In JML, side-effect free method labeled as *pure* can be used within a specification.

Unlike Dafny, the model can be implemented in JML using abstract methods that require no implementation. An advantage of the JML language is its tight connection with the Java language which makes it potentially easier for programmers to learn.

7.4.2.2   Module (2): Individual Service Contracts

The individual service contracts in JML are defined in a spec file. A spec file is a file containing the methods signatures and the specifications for a class whose implementation is not available. Listing 7.5 is the JML specification of the *SetExpressCheckout* service. In the service specification, some assertions are added to eliminate verifier warnings and errors caused by null values (e.g. lines 3, 4, 7).

7.4.2.3   Module (3): The Global Contract

Listing 7.6 is the implementation of the PayPal Express Checkout flow along with its data contract using the JML language. The flow returns the payer information on success and a null string on failure.

7.4.3   Verification Results

We used the ESC/JAVA2 [67] static checker to verify the JML implementation.[1] The tool verifies some assertions but fails however to verify the assertions at lines 4 and 10 due to limitations of the automatic theorem prover. Some of the prover

```
1  /*@ modifies ppdm, rec, token;
2   @ requires rec != null;
3   @ ensures rec != null;
4   @ ensures rec.token != null;
5   @ ensures rec.token == this.token;
6   @ ensures this.token != null;
7   @ ensures (\old(ppdm).findRecordByKey(rec.token) == null);
8   @ ensures rec.payerInfo != null;
9   @ ensures rec.transAmount == \old(sPaymentAmount);
10  @ ensures ppdm.findRecordByKey(this.token).payerInfo != null;
11  @ ensures \result == rec.token;
12  @ ensures this.token == \result;
13  @ ensures rec.paymentStatus == "InProgress";
14  @ ensures ppdm == \old(ppdm).createRecord(rec);
15  @*/
16 public String setExpressCheckout(int sPaymentAmount);
```

Listing 7.5 The specification of the *SetExpressCheckout* service in JML

---

[1] Results are generated using ESC/Java2 version 2.0.5 (Released 5 November 2008).

```
1  //@ modifies api.ppdm, api.rec, token;
2  //@ requires api != null;
3  //@ ensures (\result == api.rec.payerInfo && \result != null &&
4  //@          api.rec.paymentStatus == "Processed") ||
5  //@          (\result == null && api.rec.paymentStatus == "Denied");
6  //@ ensures \result != null ==> \result == api.rec.payerInfo &&
7  //@          api.rec.paymentStatus == "Processed";
8  //@ ensures api.rec.transAmount == \old(paymentAmount);
9  //@ ensures api.ppdm == \old(api.ppdm).createRecord(api.rec);
10
11 public String expressCheckoutFlow(float paymentAmount){
12   String returnValue = null;
13   token = api.setExpressCheckout(paymentAmount);
14   String payerInfo = api.getExpressCheckout(token);
15   boolean responseValue = api.doExpressCheckout(token, paymentAmount);
16   if(responseValue){
17     returnValue = payerInfo;
18   }
19   return returnValue;
20 }
```

Listing 7.6 The JML implementation and specification of the PayPal Express Checkout flow

Table 7.2 The verification results using the JML verifier

Method/function	Verification time (s)	Verification result
Class PayPalDM	0.016	Passed successfully
Class TransRecord	0.063	Passed successfully
ExpressCheckoutFlow	1.327	Passed successfully
Program Interpretation	0.812	
Total	2.218	

limitations are discussed in [67]. With these assertions commented out and after some code simplifications, other assertions can be verified. The verification results are shown in Table 7.2.

7.5 RESOLVE

7.5.1 The Language Design

The authors of [65] present the RESOLVE language and its verifying compiler. RESOLVE is used to write specified object-oriented code and provides tools for both generating the verification conditions and proving simple ones. The compiler has been recently implemented as a Web tool [77].

We give here a brief description of the language, its structure and tools. A tutorial can also be found at [78]. The language has its built-in specifications that are written using universal mathematical notations. The RESOLVE compiler translates the code and the specification into Java code that can be compiled using Java compiler. The language is based on mathematical theories of programming data types such as integers, strings and booleans. These theories are used in writing the formal specifications and verifying them. In addition to the theories, RESOLVE supports different types of code units. A *Concept* in RESOLVE defines the mathematical model of a data structure. For example, a stack in RESOLVE is mathematically modeled as a sequence of strings. The stack *Concept* specifies operations such as pop, push and depth. An *Enhancement* is used to add custom functionalities. For example, an *Enhancement* can be used to add a stack reverse operation to the stack *Concept*. Both *Concept* and *Enhancement* units do not provide an implementation; they only provide the specifications. A *Realization* unit on the other hand provides the implementation of a *Concept* or an *Enhancement*. This organization of RESOLVE units enables decoupling the implementation from the specification.

7.5.2   Implementation Details

In the following, we show how we use these different units to implement and specify the PayPal express checkout flow. First, Listing 7.7 is a RESOLVE Concept for the PayPal data model. In the Concept, a PayPal record is modeled as the Cartesian product of a string representing the token, an integer representing the payment status, a string representing the payer information and an integer representing the transaction amount. Already, we can see some simplifications of the model in order to use the data types provided by the language. For example, the payment status is ideally an enumeration but we use integers here instead. Constraints can be defined on a mathematical model as shown in the figure. For example, the transaction amount has to be a non-negative value. *PPDM* is a global variable representing the PayPal database and is modeled as the power set of PayPal record. The three PayPal checkout operations are specified in terms of their inputs, output and their effect on the database global variable.

RESOLVE defines a set of parameter modes. The ones we use are explained below. The full list can be found in [78].

preserves—the value of the incoming value will be preserved.
replaces—value will be replaced by some other variable.
updates—the value will be changed in an unspecified way.

The Express Checkout flow is specified using the *Enhancement* module shown in Listing 7.8. The Enhancement module specifies the flow in terms of its pre/post-conditions and frame properties. Listing 7.9 shows the corresponding implementation of the flow.

7.5.3   Verification Results

To verify that the Express Checkout implementation satisfies its specification, we first use the RESOLVE compiler to generate Verification Conditions (VCs). The VCs are a series of logical implications such that proving these implications is necessary and sufficient to demonstrate that the implementation is correct [79].

```
1  Concept PayPal_DM_Set; uses Std_Integer_Fac, Modified_String_Theory,
   Std_Boolean_Fac, Set_Theory, Std_Char_Str_Fac;
2
3    Type Family PayPal_Record is modeled by Cart_Prod
4                       Token: Char_Str;
5              Payment_Status: Integer;
6              Payer_Info: Char_Str;
7                       Trans_Amount: Integer;
8       end;
9         exemplar R;
10        constraints R.Trans_Amount >= 0 and
11          (for all Ri: PayPal_Record,  if Ri/= R then Ri.Token /= R.Token) and
12          -- Payment_Status is enumeration modeled here using integers
13          -- 0 = 'denied', 1 = 'in-progress', 2 = 'processed'
14          (R.Payment_Status = 0 or R.Payment_Status = 1 or R.Payment_Status = 2 );
15        initialization ensures R.Token /= empty_string;
16
17   Type Family PayPal_DB is modeled by Powerset(PayPal_Record);
18       exemplar db;
19        constraints true;
20        initialization ensures true;
21
22   Var Rec: PayPal_Record;
23   Var PPDM: PayPal_DB;
24
25   operation Set_Express_Checkout(preserves sPayment_Amount: Integer;
26                                   updates return:Char_Str);
27       updates PPDM, Rec;
28       ensures Rec.Token /= empty_string
29          and Rec is_not_in #PPDM
30          and Rec is_in PPDM
31          and Rec.Payer_Info /= empty_string
32          and Rec.Trans_Amount = sPayment_Amount
33          and Rec.Payment_Status = 1
34          and return = Rec.Token
35          and PPDM = Singleton(Rec) union #PPDM;
36
37   operation Get_Express_Checkout_Details(preserves gToken: Char_Str;
38                                   replaces answer: Char_Str);
39       preserves PPDM, Rec;
40       requires Rec is_in PPDM and Rec.Token = gToken;
41       ensures answer = Rec.Payer_Info;
42
43   operation Do_Express_Checkout(preserves dToken: Char_Str;
44                                 preserves dPayment_Amount: Integer;
45                                 updates return:Boolean);
46       updates PPDM, Rec;
47       requires Rec is_in PPDM and Rec.Token = dToken;
48       ensures ((return = true and Rec.Payment_Status = 2 )
49               or (return = false and Rec.Payment_Status = 0 ))
50          and Rec.Token = #Rec.Token
51          and Rec.Payer_Info = #Rec.Payer_Info
52          and Rec.Trans_Amount = dPayment_Amount
53          and PPDM = #PPDM without Singleton(#Rec) union Singleton(Rec);
54 end PayPal_DM_Set;
```

Listing 7.7 A RESOLVE concept specifying the PayPal data model and Express Checkout operations

The RESOLVE compiler generates the VCs in a user-friendly format that facilitates human inspection. They can also be generated in a syntax accepted by the Isabelle proof assistant [68] or the RESOLVE integrated prover.

Given an assertion and an implementation, the RESOLVE verifier applies proof rules, replacing code with mathematical assertions and applying some simplifications. Assuming the soundness of the proof system, if the final assertion can be reduced to true, this implies that the first assertion is correct and hence the implementation satisfies the assertion.

```
1  Enhancement PayPal_Express_Checkout_Set for PayPal_DM_Set;
2
3      Operation Express_Checkout_Flow(preserves Payment: Integer;
4                                       replaces Result: Char_Str);
5          updates PPDM, Rec;
6          ensures Rec.Trans_Amount = Payment
7              and ((Rec.Payment_Status = 2 and  Result = Rec.Payer_Info)
8                                      or (Rec.Payment_Status = 0))
9              and PPDM =  #PPDM union Singleton(Rec)
10             and Rec.Payer_Info /= empty_string;
11
12 end PayPal_Express_Checkout_Set;
```

Listing 7.8 A RESOLVE enhancement specifying the PayPal Express Checkout composition

```
1  Realization Express_Checkout_Realiz_Set for PayPal_Express_Checkout_Set
2                                          of PayPal_DM_Set;
3
4      Procedure Express_Checkout_Flow(preserves Payment: Integer;
5                                       replaces Result: Char_Str);
6
7          Var Return_Value: Char_Str;
8          Var Transaction_Token: Char_Str;
9          Var Response_Value: Boolean;
10
11         Set_Express_Checkout(Payment, Transaction_Token);
12         Get_Express_Checkout_Details(Transaction_Token, Return_Value);
13         Do_Express_Checkout(Transaction_Token, Payment, Response_Value);
14
15         If (Response_Value) then
16             Result := Return_Value;
17          end;
18
19      end Express_Checkout_Flow;
20 end Express_Checkout_Realiz_Set;
```

Listing 7.9 A RESOLVE realization providing the implementation of the PayPal Express Checkout composition

A total of 14 VCs are generated by RESOLVE verifier for our case study. One of the generated VCs is the postcondition: Rec.Trans_Amount = Payment. By applying proof rules, this assertion is reduced to payment = payment which can be trivially proven to be true. Hence, the VC can be proven to be true.

7.6 Analysis and Discussion

In this section, we discuss our experience using the three specification languages and analyze the differences and similarities among them.

7.6.1 Language Constructs

First, to implement the data model, the language that we use must allow defining a specification-only variable representing the model. Both Dafny and JML provide ghost variables for this purpose. Ghost variables are theory-typed variables that are defined only for specification purposes. RESOLVE doesn't have the explicit notion of global ghost variables; any variable in RESOLVE that is mathematically founded can be used in the specification.

To define and specify the data operations, the language must also support mathematical functions, or side-effect free methods, that can be used in the specifications. Dafny's mathematical functions are used for that purpose. The body of a mathematical function in Dafny defines its postconditions. Consequently, we had to implement the data operations using Dafny's functions instead of simply specifying them as originally intended. Once defined however, these implementations can be easily reused across different models. JML on the other hand conveniently provide *spec* files where interface-only methods can be defined and specified using JML assertions. RESOLVE provide a similar approach through the use of *Concepts* which also define interface-only methods. It's worth noting here that we made some trials to implement our model using Spec#, however, the language is lacking the necessary constructs to define theory types and hence we could not use it to define the data model.

7.6.2 Verification Process

Out of the three languages, RESOLVE is the only one that provides a human-readable form of the Verification Conditions. This enables a programmer to inspect the VCs and detect any specification error or discover assertions that may be proven true but does not reflect the programmer's intentions. The VCs generation component of RESOLVE is both sound and complete [29, 80]. The verification component of RESOLVE is still evolving and can currently be used to prove some of the simple VCs. The component is both sound and complete. On the other hand, the verification process of both JML and Dafny is neither sound nor complete due to limitations in the current implementations of the verifier. For example, we have intentionally introduced errors in the Dafny implementations and the verifier failed to detect these errors. Similarly, the verification process in JML failed to verify the implementation when a control flow statement is introduced as the verification space grows beyond the verifier capabilities.

7.6.3 Tools

Dafny uses the Boogie verifier which is a command-line tool. It is also integrated with the Visual Studio IDE to provide a real-time checking of assertions. This enables detecting programming errors while coding. A Web interface is also available to try the language and its verifier on simple examples [81]. The language does not have yet a compiler and hence programs written in Dafny can only be verified but not executed.

There are many tools that are built to compile and verify JML code; a list is provided in [82]. We use ESC/Java2 as it is relatively matured compared to other tools and has an active community and a discussion forum. JML verification tools however have limited capabilities. They support a subset of the JML language and they don't work with recent versions of Java, specifically with generics. Currently, there's an effort to develop a new generation of tools, called OpenJML, that is based on OpenJDK and support recent versions of Java [83]. An Integrated Verification Environment is presented in [84].

Finally, RESOLVE provides both a command-line tool and a Web interface compiler/verifier. The Web interface is particularly convenient to use and provide some sample code and some *Concepts* that can be adapted and reused. The RESOLVE compiler transforms the code into Java and can be used to generate the VCs for inspection. Using the Web tool, a realization can be marked with VCs, at approximate places, so that the user can connect the VCs with the code [77].

7.6.4   Learning Curve

We share here our experience in using the three languages in terms of ease of use and learning the language constructs. Table 7.3 summarizes the differences and similarities among the three languages: Dafny, JML and RESOLVE.

The Dafny language is relatively easy to learn since it has very limited set of constructs. The language combines both procedural and functional programming and hence familiarity with both is needed in order to use the language effectively. Dafny supports a limited set of data types and hence it's the programmer's responsibility to compose these types into complex ones, when needed.

JML is easy to learn for Java programmers as it uses similar syntax and is well integrated with the Java language. It defines a set of theory types that the programmer needs to learn.

Table 7.3 Comparison of the three specification languages; Dafny, JML and RESOLVE

	Dafny + Boogie	JML + ESC/Java2	RESOLVE
VCs generation soundness	No	No	Yes
VCs generation completeness	No	No	Yes
VCs inspection	No	No	Yes
Global specification variables	Yes	Yes	No
Expressiveness	Low	High	High
Compiler	No	Yes	Yes
Ease of learning	Easiest	Average	Hardest
Integration with existing programming language	None	Java	None (code can be translated to Java)

RESOLVE defines its own syntax and program structure and hence its learning curve is steep relative to Dafny and JML. The syntax has some similarity with Ada and Pascal and may therefore be easier to learn for programmers who are familiar with these languages. RESOLVE defines mathematical model and related theories for simple programming types such as integers, floats, booleans and strings that can be easily reused. Many examples are also provided through the Web tool including the implementation and specification of basic data structures such arrays, stacks and queues.

7.7 Conclusions

In this chapter, we present our effort in implementing a data model and contracting framework for Web services using state-of-the-art specification languages. Our experiment shows some limitations in current languages and formal verification techniques. However, we are able to verify some of the correctness properties using the current tools. While the current verification tools are not well suited yet for general and complex programs, there has been a significant progress in this area. Some recent efforts aim at integrating specification techniques into current mainstream programming languages, the C# contracts are an example. While they still lack the necessary constructs for defining abstract data types and tools for verifying complex assertions, they are however useful in detecting some logical errors in the code and enhancing automatic testing [85].

Chapter 8
Evaluation Using a Deep Web Case Study

Abstract We carry an experiment to test the effectiveness of our data model in reducing ambiguity about a Web service behavior. The experiment uses a Web crawling scenario. Our evaluation is based on the observation that the more queries the crawler has to try to retrieve the same set of data records, the more ambiguous the service behavior.

8.1 Experiment Description

The Deep Web refers to online data that is hidden behind dynamically generated sites and hence cannot be crawled or indexed by search engines. It is estimated that 80 % of the content on the Web is dynamically generated. With the increasing use of Web Services as gateways to online databases, data can be automatically queried and indexed by search engines by automatically invoking the corresponding services. We extracted from [86] a set of goals for effectively and efficiently crawling the Deep Web (Fig. 8.1). We consider Amazon's repository as part of the hidden Web and demonstrate how our specification for *ItemSearch* service helps achieve each of the crawler goals.

- Goal 1: Identifying services that are candidates for crawling data. Such services are typically read-only, either for any inputs or under certain input conditions. In the later case, these input conditions should be identifiable by the Web crawler.

    The *ItemSearch* service can be easily identified as read-only under any inputs since our specification does not contain any delete/create/update operations.
- Goal 2: Balancing the trade-off between trying fewer queries on the online database and maximizing the returned result set. This is achieved by enabling only relevant queries to be formulated by a crawler.

    When an input can have different values, the crawler can consult our model to automatically identify the relevant set of values that will maximize the result set. For example, as shown in Listing 6.1, the *searchIndex* input can have four different values but setting it to All (case 3) maximize the result set since the filtering set *searchIndices* will contain all possible item categories *{Book, CD, DVD}*.

© Springer International Publishing Switzerland 2015

I. Saleh, *Formalizing Data-Centric Web Services*, Web-Scale Workflow and Analytics, DOI 10.1007/978-3-319-24678-9_8

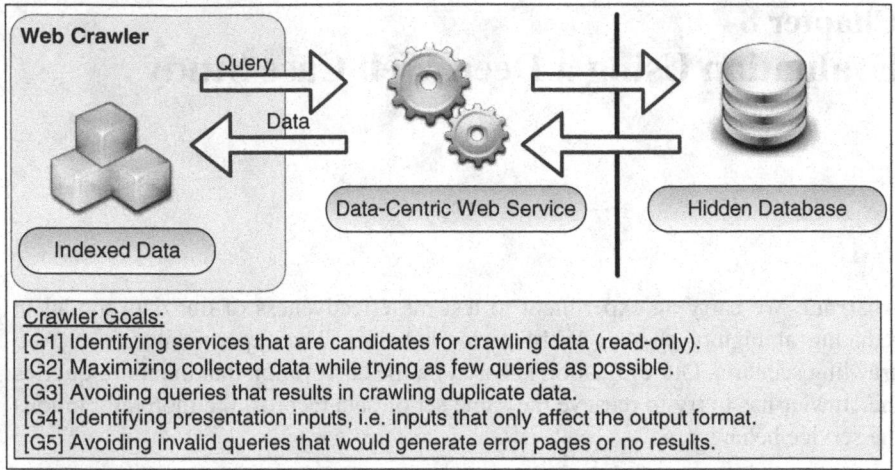

Fig. 8.1 Crawling the deep Web

– Goal 3: A service should be invoked with inputs that would potentially return
  distinct sets of records to avoid crawling duplicate data.
     The crawler can automatically reason about the filtering criteria under differ-
  ent inputs. For example, a search for books by keywords (case 2) includes both
  a search by title (case 4) and by author (case 5). Consequently, if a search by
  keywords is performed, the same search using the title or the author will not
  return new results.
– Goal 4: Identifying presentation inputs, i.e. inputs that only affect the output
  presentation like for example a parameter representing a sorting criteria. Different
  values for these presentation inputs will actually retrieve the same results.
     Presentation inputs can be identified in our model as those inputs that do not
  affect the filtering sets. The sort input is an example.
– Goal 5: Avoiding invalid inputs that would generate error pages.
     Invalid inputs can be identified from the preconditions like in line 1 of the
  specification. They can also be identified from the model invariant.

We next evaluate our model success in decreasing the level of ambiguity about
the service behavior. Our evaluation is based on the observation that the more queries the crawler has to try to retrieve the same set of data records, the more ambiguous the service behavior. Consequently, we consider the total number of possible
input combinations (queries) as an indication of the level of ambiguity of the service
specification. Our goal is to minimize the total number of input combinations by
only considering the relevant ones.

It should be noted that, to retrieve the maximum set of records, the crawler has to
try *all* possible queries, which is an NP-complete problem. We are using our model
to enable retrieval of the same data records using a filtered set of queries. While our
approach does not enhance the asymptotic complexity, it provides a significant pruning

Table 8.1 Possible values for each input parameter of the *ItemSearch* Web Service

Input parameter	Possible values	# of values
searchIndex	Books, CD, DVD, All	4
minPrice	Min, max, Nil	3
maxPrice	Min, max, Nil	3
Keywords	2 Free Text strings, Nil	3
author	2 Free Text strings, Nil	3
Artist	2 Free Text strings, Nil	3
Title	2 Free Text strings, Nil	3
Merchant	2 Free Text strings, Nil	3
Availability	Available, Nil	2
Sort	price, -price	2

of the number of queries that need to be executed against the data source. We use the number of pruned queries as an indication of our model effectiveness in decreasing ambiguity.

8.2   Methodology

Table 8.1 shows the inputs of the *ItemSearch* service and their possible values. We assume the crawler can generate two values for each of the free text inputs using the technique in. We also assume that a *min* and a *max* values are selected for the *min-Price* and *maxPrice* inputs, respectively, and each of them can also be set to Nil.

8.3   Independent Variable

The experiment is carried on through steps where we incrementally build the data contract of the service by adding assertions at each step. We then measure the level of ambiguity in the service behavior at each of these steps. The goal is to measure the effect of the degree of sophistication of the contract on demystifying the data interactions implemented by a service.

8.4   Dependent Variable

Measuring the level of ambiguity about the service behavior is a very subjective matter. Alternatively, we use our observation, stated before, that the more queries the crawler has to try to retrieve the same set of data records, the more ambiguous the service behavior. We hence consider the total number of possible input combinations (queries) as an indication of the level of ambiguity of the service specification. We calculate the total number of these queries at each level of sophistication of the data contract.

8.5 Results and Analysis

Table 8.2 summarizes the effect of the contract specification level on the number of query formulated. Levels are defined in terms of number of assertions from Listing 6.1 that are used to annotate the service. Levels are cumulative. The results are depicted in Fig. 8.2.

Table 8.2 Number of possible queries for each service specification level

Specification level	Number of queries	Queries filtering criterion
L0:No specifications	$4*3^7*2^2 = \mathbf{34,992}$	None (some of these queries are invalid)
L1:Lines 1–4	$4*8*3^5*2^2 = \mathbf{31,104}$	Excluding queries that have *minPrice* > *maxPrice* since they violate the precondition
L2:Lines 5–33	$1*8*2*1^3*3*2^2 = \mathbf{192}$	Only case 3 is considered to return maximum number of records, case 1, 2, and 4 will generate duplicates
L3:Lines 34–46	$1*8*2*1^3*3*1*2 = \mathbf{96}$	Excluding queries where *itemAvailability* is set to Available since it has a more strict filtering set
L4:Lines 47–52	$1*8*2*1^4*2 = \mathbf{32}$	*merchantName* default value is used to ensure results are returned
L5:Lines 53–66	$1*8*2*1^6 = \mathbf{16}$	The sort input is identified as a representation parameter

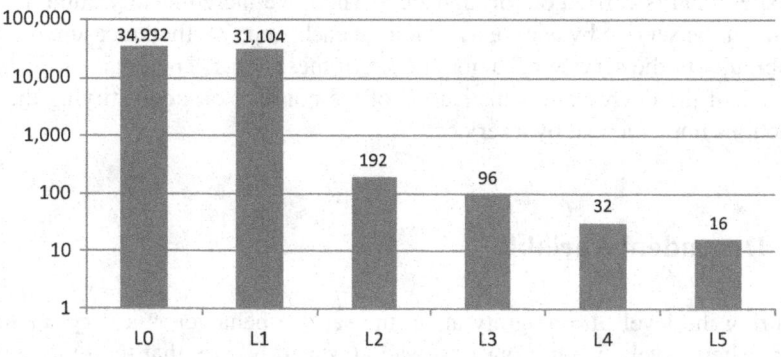

Fig. **8.2** Number of possible queries for *ItemSearch* service with different levels of specifications

The *ItemSearch* crawling logic is implemented as a constraint satisfaction problem using constraint logic programming (CLP) in Prolog [87]. The service data contract is implemented as set of constraints. The solution of the constraint satisfaction problem in this case is a set of service queries that satisfy both the contract constraints and the crawling goals listed in Fig. 8.2. We have implemented the first three levels of specification using Prolog and collected the corresponding number of possible queries. The Prolog code is included in Appendix B. The numbers of queries at levels L3–L5 are manually calculated based on corresponding query filtering criterion.

The results indicate that the service contract has a great impact on narrowing the search space for queries and consequently promoting the service understandability and reusability. By complying with the service contract, the crawler is also guaranteed to invoke the service using valid inputs that will not generate errors and that will maximize the result set.

Chapter 9
Static Detection of Implementation Errors Using Code Contracts

Abstract The experiment described in this chapter is performed in order to test our hypothesis that formal code contracts enables detection of programming errors at design time. We use mutation testing techniques in order to evaluate the effectiveness of the code contracts at different level of contract sophistication.

9.1 Experiment Description

Formal specifications are a set of assertions added to a piece of code to represent the programmer's intentions. A tool that statically verifies the correctness of the code with respect to these assertions is called a *verifying compiler*. The input and output of a verifying compiler is shown in Fig. 9.1. The input is a set of mathematical specifications and code that is intended to implement those specifications. A compiler performs standard checks—such as syntax and type checking—on both the code and the specs, and then a verifier attempts to prove that the code correctly implements the specifications.

We investigate the impact of various levels of formal specification on the ability to statically detect errors in code. Our goal is to quantify the return on investment with regards to the effectiveness of identifying errors versus the overhead of specifying software at various levels of detail. We looked at thirteen common algorithms and data structures implemented using C# and specified using Spec#. We selectively omitted various parts of the specification to come up with five different levels of specification, from unspecified to highly-specified.

We adapt a methodology from the software testing fields where code mutation is used to assess the quality of a testing technique. Mutation testing [88–90] is carried out by injecting errors in the code and measuring the ability of a testing tool to detect these errors. The main assumption with this methodology is that the number of mutation errors detected by a tool is an indication of number of errors that this tool can detect in the future when unknown bugs are present in the code. We use a similar methodology to evaluate the ability of code specification in detecting mutation errors. In our experiment we use a set of mutation operators that are based on the Mothra mutation testing system [91]. Mothra defines a set of mutation operators derived from studies of programmers' errors and correspond to mistakes that programmers typically make. This set of operators represent more than 10 years of

© Springer International Publishing Switzerland 2015
I. Saleh, *Formalizing Data-Centric Web Services*, Web-Scale Workflow and Analytics, DOI 10.1007/978-3-319-24678-9_9

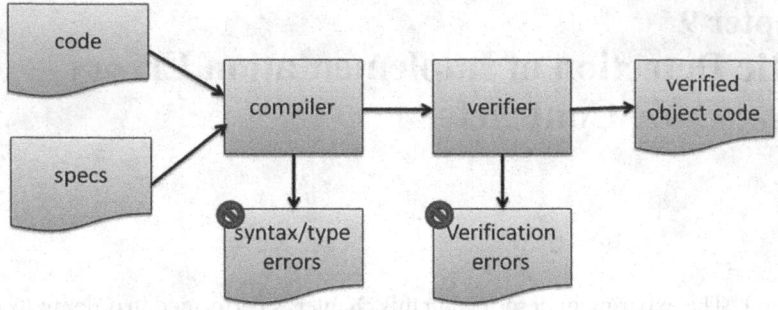

Fig. 9.1 Input and output of a verifying compiler

refinement through several mutation systems [88]. The authors of [92] further extend these operators to support C# object orientation and syntax. They also present in [93] an empirical study that evaluates the quality of these mutation operators and establish their relationship to actual programmers' errors. We use the tool that they provide in our experiment.

We choose Spec# as our specification language as it represents a recent effort of integrating formal specification with current programming practices. Spec# uses constructs with similar syntax to the C# programming language. Consequently, it is easier for programmers to learn the languages over other specification languages that use special-purpose mathematical notations. We also use the Boogie [74] verifier for Spec#. Boogie is a static verifier that uses a theorem prover to verify that a program or class satisfies its specification. We consider different constructs that are used to write code specification. In the following paragraphs, we describe each construct along with examples that we adapt from [17]. The examples are written using Spec# syntax.

9.1.1   Non-null Types

This construct is used to denote whether an expression may or may not evaluate to null. Such a mechanism helps programmers avoid null-dereference errors. The following class declares an attribute t as a non-null type by using the exclamation point (!). Hence, the class constructor needs to assign a non-null value to *t*.

```
class Student : Person {
    Transcript! t;
    public Student (string name, EnrollmentInfo! ei): base(name) {
        t = new Transcript(ei);
}
```

9.1.2 Method Contracts

Every method can have a specification that describes its use, outlining a contract between callers and implementations. Method contracts establish responsibilities, from which one can assign blame in case of a contract violation error [17]. Method contracts consist of preconditions, postconditions, and frame conditions.

Preconditions specify the conditions under which the method is allowed to be called. Here is a simple example:

```
class ArrayList {
    public virtual void Insert(int index, object value)
    requires 0 <= index && index <= Count;
    {. . .}
}
```

The precondition is written using a *requires* clause and specifies that the index into which the object is to be inserted in the array list must be within bounds.

Postconditions specify under which conditions the method is allowed to return. For example, the postconditions of *Insert* can be specified as follows:

```
ensures Count == old(Count) + 1;
ensures value == this[index];
ensures Forall{int i in 0 : index; old(this[i]) == this[i]};
```

These postconditions are written using *ensures* clauses and they state that the effect of *Insert* is to increase *Count* by 1, to insert the given value at the given index, and to keep all other elements in their same relative positions. In the first line, **old**(*Count*) denotes the value of *Count* on entry to the method. In the third line, the special function *Forall* is applied to the comprehension of the boolean expression *old(this[i])* == *this[i]*, where *i* ranges over the integer values in the half-open interval from 0 to less than index.

Frame Conditions limit the parts of the program state that the method is allowed to modify. In the following class code for example, method *M* is permitted to have a net effect on the value of *x*, whereas the value of *y* on exit from the method must have the same value as on entry.

```
class C {
    int x, y;
    void M() modifies x; {. . .}
}
```

9.1.3   Class Contracts

These specifications are called object invariants and spell out what is expected to
hold for each object's data fields in the steady state of the object [17]. For example,
the following class fragment declares that the lengths of the arrays students and
absent are to be the same.

```
class AttendanceRecord {
    Student[]! students;
    bool[]! absent;
    invariant students.Length == absent.Length;
}
```

9.1.4   Loop Invariants

These invariants are logical assertions that must evaluate to true at the beginning
and end of every iteration of the loop. The following code fragment shows an example of a loop invariant.

```
for (int n = i; n < j; n++)
   invariant i <= n && n <= j; {
   s += a[n];
}
```

9.1.5   Assertions

Assertions are Boolean expressions that specify assumptions within a piece of code.
Assertions are typically checked at runtime, however, they can also be used to help
a code verifier statically prove that some other code conditions hold. An example is
shown below.

```
public int doubler(int x){
    int XX;
    XX = 2 * x;
    assert XX == 2 * x;
    return XX;
}
```

9.2 Data Set

For the purpose of our experiment, we consider a set of 13 formally specified C#
classes. These classes are implemented and formally specified by the authors of [94]
based on a collection of textbook algorithms provided in [95]. The authors use
Spec# to annotate the C# code with formal assertions. The data set represents a set
of general-purpose algorithms including search and sort algorithms, basic data
structures, mathematical calculations and array manipulation functionalities. The
classes are selected as a set of simple yet practical examples of using code specifications. Our population consists of the whole set of 13 classes without prior filtering
or changes in the specifications originally added by their implementers. Table 9.1
lists the 13 classes along with short descriptions of their functionalities

Note that classes 4 and 5 represent the same implementation of the Bubble Sort
algorithm but with different specifications. The specification writers used this example to demonstrate different ways to express the same assertion using different Spec#
constructs. We use this example in the experiment to give an insight into the effect of
different specifications on the ability to discover errors, as will be detailed later.

9.3 Methodology

We test our hypothesis by applying the following steps:

1. Each class in Table 1.1 is verified using the Boogie verifier to ensure that the
   implementation initially satisfies the formal specifications.

Table 9.1 The experiment's data set

No.	Class	Description
1	CircQueue	Circular array implementation of Queue
2	IntStack	Non-Circular array implementation of Stack
3	ArrayCount	Calculates the number of nulls in an array
4	BubbleSort1	Implements the Bubble Sort to sort an array of integers
5	BubbleSort2	Implements the Bubble Sort to sort an array of integers
6	SegmentSum	Calculates the sum of the elements in an array segment
7	DutchNationalFlag	Given 'N' objects colored red, white or blue, sorts them so that objects of the same color are adjacent, with the colors in the order red, white and blue
8	GCD	Calculates the Greatest Common Divisor of two numbers
9	SumXValues	Sum the first x numbers in an array
10	Reverse	Reverses the order of elements in an array
11	Queue	Non-Circular array implementation of Queue
12	BinarySearch	Implements the Binary Search to determine if an element is in an array
13	SumEven	Sums values at the even indices of an array

Table 9.2 Mutation operators used in the experiment

No.	Operator	Description	Example
1	AOR	Arithmetic operator replacement	a=b+c *to* a=b−c
2	ROR	Relational operator replacement	while(a<b) *to* while (a>b)
3	PRV	Reference assignment with other compatible type	a=b *to* a=c
4	EOC	Replace == with Equals()	x==0 *to* x.Equals(0)
5	JID	Member variable initialization deletion	int[] a=new int[2] *to* int[] a
6	JTD	*This* keyword deletion	This.x *to* x

2. A fault injection tool, implemented by the authors of [89], is used to automatically introduce errors in each class. Software fault injection techniques are described in [96] and the authors of [89] extend these techniques for object-oriented code. These techniques simulate programmer errors by randomly applying mutation operators. A subset of these mutation operators is used in our experiment and we describe them in Table 9.2.
3. The Boogie verifier is executed on each mutant of each class. If the verifier generates an error, than the mutant is said to be *killed* and the specification has enabled the error to be detected. Otherwise, the error has not been detected by the automatic verifier and the mutant is said to be *alive*.
4. Step (3) is repeated for different types of errors and the total number of errors detected using different specification levels is calculated.

The following specification levels are considered in the experiment:

- L0: No specification, this level acts as a baseline
- L1: Specifying only the non-null types
- L2: Adding assertions and both loop and class invariants to L1 specifications
- L3: Specifying only the methods preconditions in addition to L1 specifications
- L4: The highest level of specification provided for a class including non-null types, methods contracts, frame conditions, class contracts, loop and class invariants and assertions.

These levels are selected from a practicality standpoint as we believe they capture the different levels of efforts that can be invested by programmers in writing formal specifications. It is worth noting here that L4 is the highest specification level provided by the specification writers and does not necessarily imply a comprehensive specification of the code behavior.

A total of 248 mutants were generated and formally verified throughout the experiment. Table 9.3 gives a summary of number of mutants generated for each class and the mutation operators that they cover.

Table 9.3 Mutation operators applied to each class and the corresponding number of mutants

No.	Class	Mutation operators	No. of mutants
1	CircQueue	AOR—ROR—EOC—JID	25
2	IntStack	ROR—EOC—JID	13
3	ArrayCount	ROR—JTD	7
4	BubbleSort1	AOR—ROR	22
5	BubbleSort2	AOR—ROR	22
6	SegmentSum	ROR	5
7	DutchNationalFlag	AOR—ROR	41
8	GCD	AOR—ROR—EOC—PRV	31
9	SumXValues	AOR—ROR	13
10	Reverse	ROR	5
11	Queue	ROR—EOC—JID	13
12	BinarySearch	AOR—ROR	35
13	SumEven	AOR—ROR—EOC—JID	16
Total			248

9.4   Independent Variable

The independent variable in the proposed experiment is the specification level. The specification level is a *nominal* variable that includes the five levels of specification L0–L4.

9.5   Depended Variable

The dependent variable is a *ratio* value capturing the percentage of errors detected to the total number of errors injected into the code. This is also called the mutation score in the software testing terminology.

The main idea is that the number of errors detected using either of the specification levels studied in our experiment is an indication of the correctness of software produced using that level. Our goal is to measure the effectiveness of the formal specification in detecting design-time errors and hence maximizing software correctness. The mutation scores are used as a measure of that effectiveness. We would also like to study the effect of each level of specification on our ability to detect different categories of errors.

9.6   Results and Analysis

9.6.1   Mutation Score

For each class used in our experiment, we calculated the mutation score at different levels of specifications. We then analyzed the results to test if there's a significant difference achieved at the different specification levels. The results are represented using the boxplot in Fig. 9.2. It should be noted here that the mutation tool generates errors that are syntactically correct and hence none of these injected errors are detected by the C# non-verifying compiler. In other words, the mutation score of the non-verifying compiler is consistently equal to zero.

Figure 9.3 presents the histogram of mutation score values for the different level of specifications.

Our next set of results calculates the mutation scores achieved at different levels of specifications for different types of mutation errors. The results are depicted in Fig. 9.4.

As seen in the figure, L4 performs the best by detecting the highest number of errors across different error types while L2 comes at the second rank. There's no significant difference between L0, L1 and L3 in their ability to detect errors. In the following subsection, we take a closer look on some of the examples where errors are not detected by the specification.

9.6.2   Observations

– Mutants that do not introduce a logical error

Some errors are not detected by any of the specification levels as shown in Fig. 9.2. Mainly, the errors of type JID (the deletion of a variable initialization) and JTD (the deletion of *this* keyword) are never detected. However, throughout

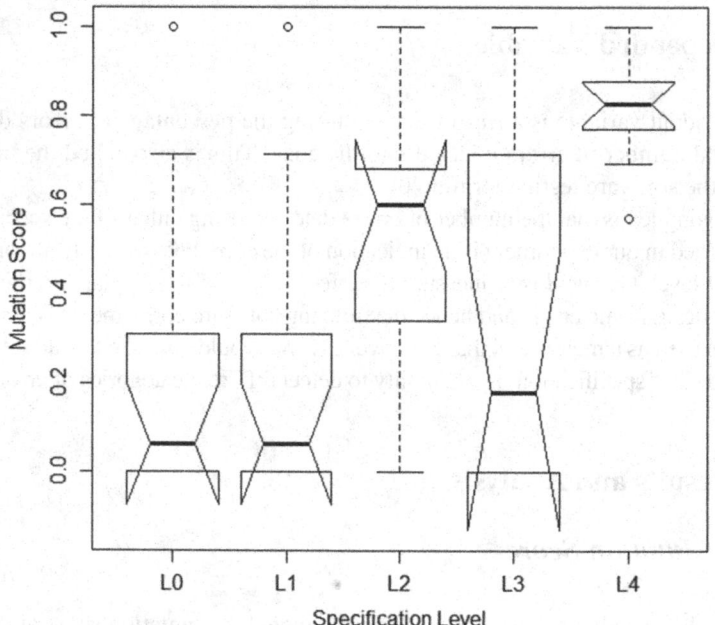

Fig. 9.2 The mutation scores achieved at different specification levels

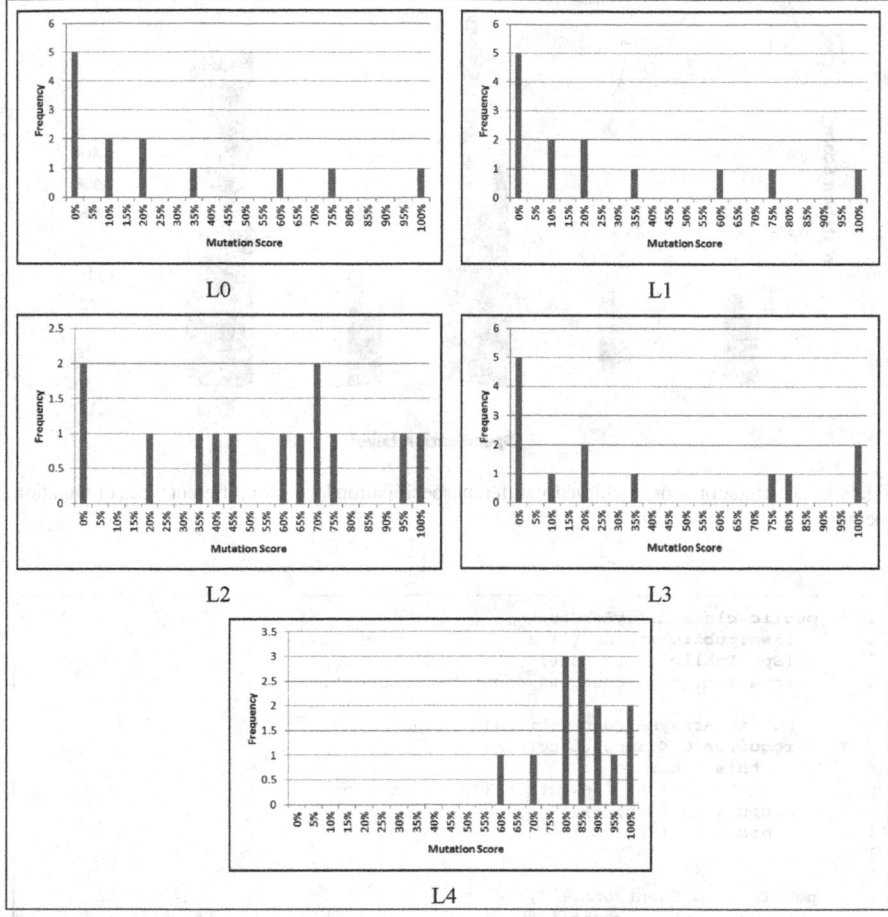

Fig. 9.3 The histograms of the mutation scores achieved at different specification levels

our experiment, all JID errors have generated a Spec# compilation warning. It should also be noted that the JTD mutation introduces an error whenever a program has a local variable and class attributes with the same name. This was not the case in our experiment and hence the mutation did not actually result in an error. An example is shown in Listing 9.1. Mutants that remove the *this* keyword on lines 8 or on line 11 are not killed by the specification as they don't constitute a logical error in this case.

– Preconditions

The results suggest that the preconditions have less ability in detecting errors than invariants and assertions. It should be noted here that a mutant is killed by a precondition if the mutation causes violation of this precondition on a method call. This case is not common in our dataset where many programs consisted of

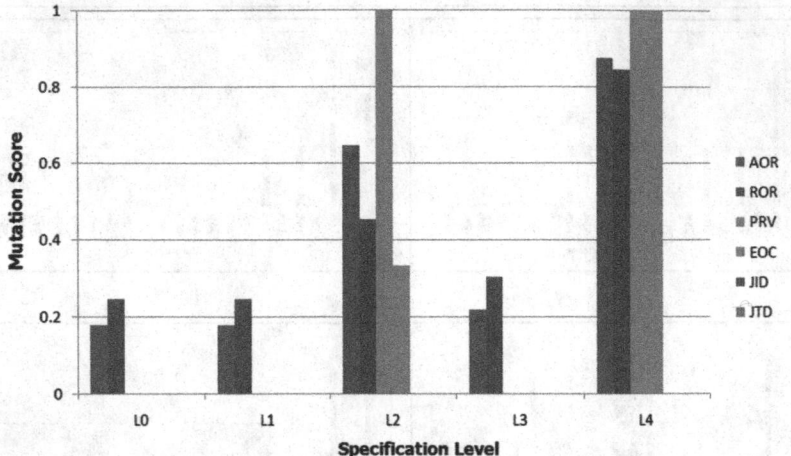

Fig. 9.4 The mutation scores achieved at different specification levels for different types of mutation operators

```
1    public class ArrayRefCount {
2      [Rep]public string []! a;
3      [SpecPublic] int count;
4      invariant 0 <= count && count <= a.Length;
5
6      public ArrayRefCount(string[]! input)
7      requires 0 < input.Length; {
8        this.count  = 0;
9        string[]! b = new string[input.Length];
10      input.CopyTo(b, 0);
11      this.a = b;
12     }
13
14     public void CountNonNull()
15     ensures count == count{int i in (0: a.Length); (a[i] != null)}; {
16       expose(this){
17       int ct = 0;
18       for (int i = 0; i < a.Length; i++)
19       invariant i <= a.Length; //infers 0<=i
20       invariant 0 <= ct && ct <= i;
21       invariant ct == count{int j in (0: i); (a[j]!=null)}; {
22         if (a[i]!=null) ct++;
23       }
24       count = ct;
25       }
26     }
27   }
```

Listing 9.1 An implementation of a class used to count number of nulls in an array

a class with one method that is not called elsewhere. This explains the high variance of the mutation score at L3. Listing 9.2 for example shows the implementation of a GCD calculator. A mutant changing line 6 to be `while (i < a-b)` is not detected by the precondition at line 4 but can be detected by the invariant as it causes violation to the assertion at line 7.

```
1    public class GCD {
2
3       static int CalculateGCD(int a, int b)
4       requires a > 0 && b > 0; {
5          int i = 1; int res = 1;
6       while (i < a+b) {
7       invariant i <= a+b;
8       invariant res > 0 && a % res == 0 && b % res == 0;
9       invariant forall{int k in (1..i), a % k == 0 && b % k == 0;
10                                                    k <= res};{
11            i++;
12         if (a % i == 0 && b % i == 0) {
13               res = i;
14         }
15       }
16       return res;
17    }
18   }
```

Listing 9.2 An implementation of a GCD calculator

- Different specification constructs

     We have also investigated a case where the same code has two different speci-
fications. The result shows a difference in the mutation score when the same
class is annotated with different loop invariants. This is depicted in Fig. 9.5
where the same implementation of the Bubble Sort algorithm has been specified
differently using two different sets of loop invariants. As shown in the figure,
there's a difference in number of error detected at L2 and L4. The corresponding
code is shown in Listing 9.3a, b. The main difference between the two sets of
invariants is the use of the relational operator <= in (a), versus using the Spec#
keyword *max* in (b) to specify that at each iteration, a segment of the array is
sorted. This issue needs more investigation to study the properties of each invariant and its effect on detecting implementation errors.
- Loop invariants

     In some cases, the loop invariants have actually concealed an error that is
detected when no invariant is added. This is due to the way the Boogie verifier
handles loop unfolding. Figure 9.6 shows two examples where loop invariants at
L2 and L4 cause some errors to be undetected by the verifier. The *ArrayCount*
invariant is shown in Listing 9.1.
- Errors undetected under the highest level of specification

     Theoretically, all mutation errors should be detected at the highest level of
specification level, L4. However, looking at the results, this is not the case. We
take a closer look at some of the cases where errors in L4 go undetected by the
Boogie verifier. Listing 9.4 for example shows the implementation of the *isFull()*
method for a queue data structure class. The queue is implemented using a static
array of integers. The *isFull()* method returns true if the tail of the queue is equal
to number of elements in the array.

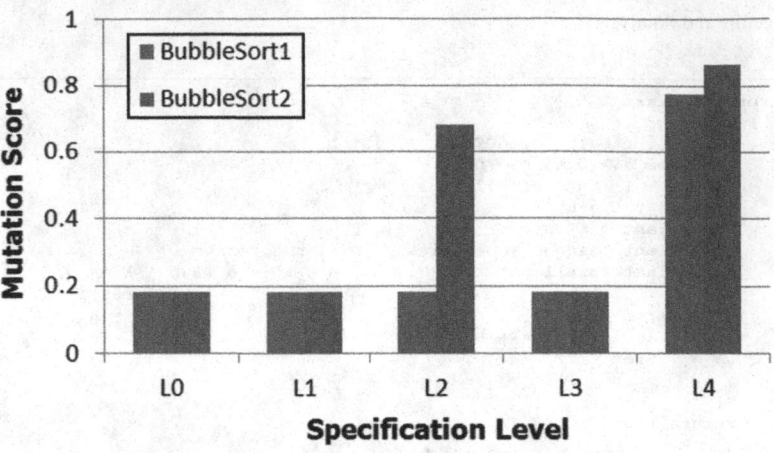

Fig. 9.5 The effect of different loop invariants on error detection

```
                                    (a)
1    public class BubbleSort1 {
2
3        static void Sort_Forall(int[]! a)
4        modifies a[*];
5        ensures forall{int i in (0: a.Length), int j in (0: a.Length),
6                                          i <= j; a[i] <= a[j]}; {
7          for (int n = a.Length; 0 <= --n; )
8          invariant 0 <= n && n <= a.Length;
9          invariant forall{int i in (n: a.Length), int k in (0: i);
10                                          a[k] <= a[i]}; {
11            for (int j = 0; j < n; j++)
12            invariant j <= n;
13            invariant forall{int i in (n+1: a.Length), int k in (0: i);
14                                          a[k] <= a[i]};
15            invariant forall{int k in (0: j); a[k] <= a[j]}; {
16              if (a[j+1] < a[j]) {
17                int tmp = a[j];   a[j] = a[j+1];   a[j+1] = tmp;
18              }
19            }
20          }
21        }
22    }
```

```
                                    (b)
1    public class BubbleSort2 {
2
3        static void Sort_Max(int[]! a)
4        modifies a[*];
5        ensures forall{int i in (0: a.Length), int j in (0: a.Length),
6                                  i <= j; a[i] <= a[j]}; {
7          for (int n = a.Length; 0 <= --n; )
8          invariant 0 <= n && n <= a.Length;
9          invariant forall{int i in (n: a.Length);
10                                 a[i] == max{int k in (0..i); a[k]}}; {
11            for (int j = 0; j < n; j++)
12            invariant j <= n;
13            invariant forall{int i in (n+1: a.Length);
14                                 a[i] == max{int k in (0..i); a[k]}};
15            invariant a[j] == max{int k in (0..j); a[k]}; {
16              if (a[j+1] < a[j]) {
17                int tmp = a[j];   a[j] = a[j+1];   a[j+1] = tmp;
18              }
19            }
20          }
21        }
22    }
```

Listing 9.3 An implementation of Bubble sort with two different sets of loop invariants

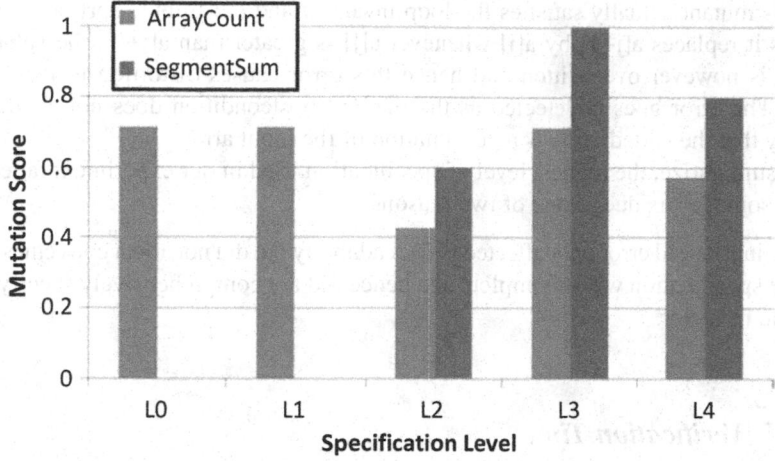

Fig. 9.6 The effect of loop invariants on error hiding

```
1    public class IntQueue {
2
3    [Rep][SpecPublic] int[]! elements = new int[10];
4    [SpecPublic] int head;
5    [SpecPublic] int tail;
6    invariant 0 <= head && head <= elements.Length;
7    invariant 0 <= tail && tail <= elements.Length;
8    invariant head <= tail;
9    ...
10    [Pure] public bool IsFull()
11    ensures result == (tail == elements.Length); {
12       return (tail == elements.Length);
13    }
14    ...
15 }
```

Listing 9.4 A code snippet of an implementation of a Queue data structure

One of the mutants generated for this class consisted of changing the return statement of the *isFull()* method at line 12 to be:

```
return (tail >= elements.Length);
```

This mutant is however not killed by the Boogie verifier. The reason is that, given the class invariant at line 7, the condition `tail >= elements.length` is equivalent to `tail == elements.length` which still satisfies the postcondition.

Another case where errors are not detected at L4 is the case when the specification is actually incomplete. Consider for example a mutant of the code in Listing 9.3b that introduces an error in the swap operation at line 17 to be:

```
int tmp = a[j];  a[j] = a[j*1];  a[j+1] = tmp;
```

This mutant actually satisfies the loop invariant and the Bubble sort postcondition as it replaces a[j+1] by a[j] whenever a[j] is greater than a[j+1], the value of a[j+1] is however overwritten and hence this error causes distortion to the input array. The error goes undetected as the method postcondition does not explicitly specify that the sorted array is a permutation of the input array.

To summarize, the highest level of specification used in our experiment failed to detect some errors due to one of two reasons:

– The introduced error only affected code readability but did not affect correctness, or
– The specification was incomplete and hence did not comprehensively specify the code behavior.

9.6.3 Verification Time

In this section, we present some performance analysis of the verification process. The goal is to show the feasibility of using a verifying-compiler. The verification times are calculated by running the Boogie verifier on Spec# programs using an Intel Core i3 CPU, 2.13 GHz machine with 4 GB RAM and 64-bit operating system. Figure 9.7 shows the boxplot for the verification time for each of the five specification levels.

As seen from the results, there's no significance difference in performance between difference specification levels. The verification time ranges between 0.08 and 0.11 s per program. Depending on the development environment, these numbers can be useful in estimating the overhead of using a verifying-compiler versus a non-verifying one.

9.6.4 Validity Discussion

In this section, we discuss some threats to our experiment both from internal and external validity standpoints.

9.6.4.1 Internal Validity

First, we used in our experiment a mutation tool implemented by the authors of [89] and [92]. Due to the structural characteristics and the rare usage of some programming constructions in some programs, the tool generates a limited number of mutants for some mutation operators. In those cases the calculated mutation scores can be treated only approximately, showing certain trends, but without sufficient statistical power [92]. Figure 9.8 shows the number of mutants that the tool generated for each mutation operator. As seen from the figure, while the tool could generate relatively large number of mutants of type ROR and AOR, it could not generate as many mutants

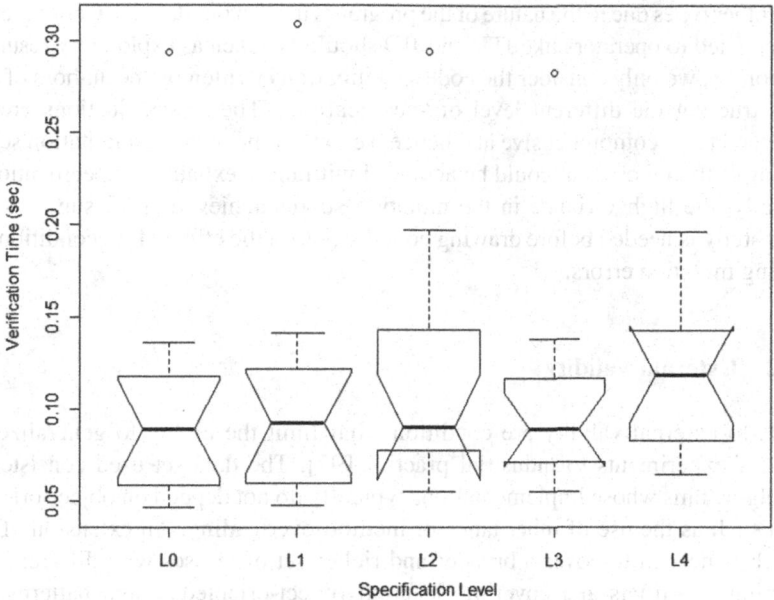

Fig. 9.7 The verification time at different specification levels

Fig. 9.8 The number of
mutants generated for each
mutation operator

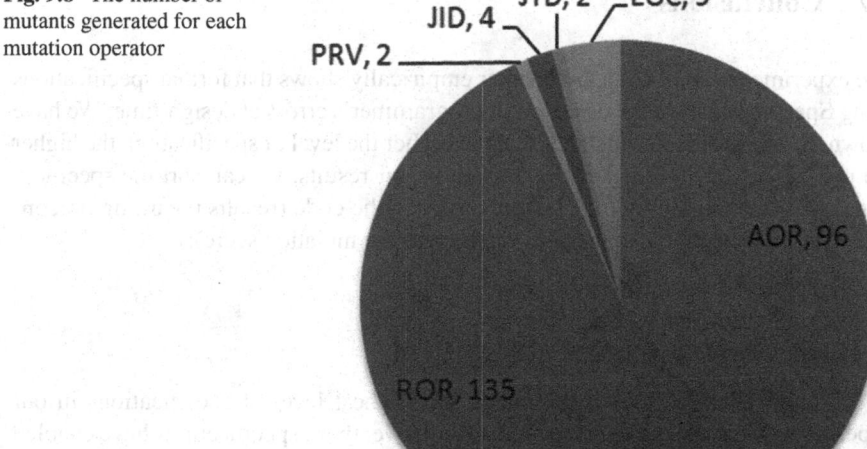

for the other types due to the nature of the programs used in our data set. Consequently, results related to operators like JTD and JID should be taken as exploratory results.

Secondly, we only consider the code specifications written by the authors of [94] in constructing the different level of specifications. These specifications are not guaranteed to be comprehensive and hence we expect the measured mutation scores to be lower than those that could be achieved with more exhaustive specifications.

Finally, the high variance in the mutation scores achieved at L3 suggests that further study is needed before drawing conclusions on the effect of preconditions on detecting mutation errors.

9.6.4.2   External Validity

Threats to external validity are conditions that limit the ability to generalize the results of experiments to industrial practice [92]. The data set used consisted of basic algorithms whose implementations typically do not depend on object-oriented design such as the use of inheritance or method overloading. An extension of this research is needed to cover a broader and richer set of classes with different programming constructs and covering different object-oriented design patterns. We have also used C# and Spec# as our programming and specification languages, respectively. Hence, care should be taken if results are to be generalized to other languages, especially if different verification techniques are used.

9.7   Conclusions

The experiment described in this chapter empirically shows that formal specifications using Spec# can enable the detection of programmer's errors at design-time. We have shown by using statistical methods that the higher the level of specification, the higher the probability of detecting errors. Based on our results, we can sort the specification levels by their ability of detecting errors in the code (results regarding precondition are indecisive due to the high variance in the mutation score):

1. The highest level of specifications
2. Invariants and 'assert' statements
3. Non-null types or no specification

It should be noted that, even though the highest level of specifications in our experiments were not guaranteed to be exhaustive, these specifications have enabled the discovery of 83 %, on average, of the injected errors. As shown in the results, some errors are detected by using a verifying-compiler without adding code specifications. This is due to the fact that a verifying-compiler applies some additional checks, e.g. array bound checking and possible divisions by zero. This can be a useful practice for developers that would like to enhance the quality of their code without adding the effort of formally specifying it.

Chapter 10
Static Detection of Implementation Errors in Data-Centric Web Services

Abstract The experiment described in this chapter is performed to test our hypothesis that our formal model and contracting framework enables detection of programming errors at design time in data-centric Web services. Again, we use mutation testing techniques in order to measure the effectiveness of the data contract attached to services.

10.1 Experiment Description

We investigate the impact of modeling and specifying data-centric services on the ability to statically detect errors in the services' code. Similar to the experiment described in Chap. 9, we apply mutation testing but this time on code modeled and specified using our proposed formal contracting framework. The number of mutation errors detected by the verifier is used as an indication of ability of our model and code contract in detecting implementation errors.

10.2 Data Set

For the purpose of our experiment, we consider a set of 17 C# functionalities extracted from a book rental application available at [97]. The application represents a CRUD application whose functionalities depend on interaction with a database. We add our model to the C# code and we use Spec# to annotate the code with formal assertions. Table 10.1 lists the databases functionalities that we model and specify for the purpose of the experiments.

10.3 Methodology

We test our hypothesis by applying the following steps:

1. A class with all the 17 functionalities is implemented. The class contains variables that represent the underlying database according to our proposed data modeling

© Springer International Publishing Switzerland 2015   95
I. Saleh, *Formalizing Data-Centric Web Services*, Web-Scale Workflow and Analytics, DOI 10.1007/978-3-319-24678-9_10

Table 10.1 The experiment's data set

No.	Functionality	Description
1	create_book	Creates a new book given the book ISBN, title, publisher and category
2	create_category	Creates a new book category given the category name
3	create_customer	Creates a new customer given the customer name
4	create_publisher	Creates a new publisher given the publisher name
5	create_user	Creates a new application administrator given a username and password
6	delete_customer	Deletes an existing customer given the customer's name
7	delete_publisher	Deletes an existing publisher given the publisher's name
8	delete_user	Deletes an existing administrator given the administrator's name
9	find_book_by_isbn	Searches for a book given an ISBN
10	find_category_by_name	Searches for a category given a name
11	find_customer_by_name	Searches for a customer given a name
12	find_publisher_by_name	Searches for a publisher given a name
13	find_user_by_username	Searches for an administrator given a username
14	purchase_book	Creates a new purchase given the book ISBN, quantity and price per book
15	rent_book	Creates a new rental given the book ISBN, rental days, price per day and customer id
16	return_book	Returns a book given an ISBN
17	update_user_password	Updates an administrator's password given a username

methodology. Due to the limitation of the Spec# and Boogie systems, we simplified our model for the purpose of this experiment as will be explained later.

2. All methods in the class are specified using Spec#. The specification defines how these methods interact with the data model variables in terms of reading and/or modifying records.

3. The specified implementation is verified using Boogie to ensure that it is initially correct with respect to the specifications.

4. A fault injection tool, implemented by the authors of [89], is used to automatically introduce errors in the class. The mutation operators that the tool applies depend on the code to be mutated, and in our case, the set of operators described in Table 10.2 are used.

5. The Boogie verifier is executed on each mutant of the class. If the verifier generates an error, than the mutant is said to be *killed* and the specification has enabled the error to be detected. Otherwise, the error has not been detected by the automatic verifier and the mutant is said to be *alive*.

6. Step (3) is repeated for different types of errors and the total number of errors detected using different specification levels is calculated.

Table 10.2 Mutation operators used in the experiment

No.	Operator	Description	Example
1	ABS	Replacing a numerical value with its absolute value	int x = y *to* int x = Math.Abs(y)
2	AOR	Arithmetic operator replacement	a=b+c *to* a=b−c
3	ROR	Relational operator replacement	while(a<b) *to* while (a>b)
4	UOI	Unary operator insertion	a=b *to* a=−b
5	UOR	Unary operator replacement	i++ *to* i−−

The following specification levels are considered in the experiment:

- L0: No specification, this level acts as a baseline
- L1: Specifying only the non-null types
- L2: Adding both loops and class invariants to L1 specifications
- L3: Specifying only the methods preconditions in addition to L1 specifications
- L4: The highest level of specification provided for a method including non-null types, frame conditions, postconditions, and both loops and class invariants.

As mentioned in Chap. 9, these levels are selected from a practicality standpoint as we believe they capture the different levels of efforts that can be invested by programmers in writing formal specifications. It is worth noting here that L4 is the highest specification level that could be added given the Spec# syntax and verification capabilities and does not necessarily imply a comprehensive specification of the code behavior.

A total of 134 mutants were generated and formally verified throughout the experiment (Fig. 10.1). Table 10.3 gives a summary of number of mutants generated for each class and the mutation operators that they cover.

10.4 Independent Variable

The independent variable in the proposed experiment is the specification level. The specification level is a *nominal* variable that includes the five levels of specification L0 to L4.

10.5 Depended Variable

The dependent variable is a *ratio* value capturing the percentage of errors detected to the total number of errors injected into the code. This is also called the mutation score in the software testing terminology. The number of errors detected using either of the specification levels studied in our experiment is an indication of the correctness of software produced using that level. Our goal is to study the effectiveness of adding our data model and formal specification in detecting design-time errors and consequently in maximizing correctness of data-centric services. The mutation scores are used as the measure of effectiveness. We would also like to study the effect of each level of specification on our ability to detect different categories of errors.

Fig. 10.1 The number of mutants generated for each mutation operator

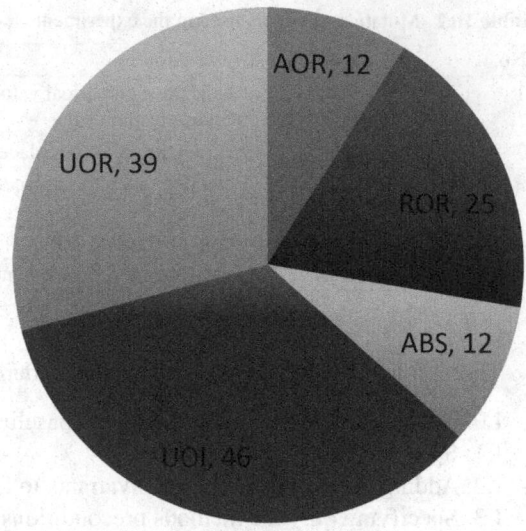

Table 10.3 Mutation operators and the corresponding number of mutants

No.	Method	Mutation operators	No. of mutants
1	create_book	UOR	3
2	create_category	UOR	3
3	create_customer	UOR	3
4	create_publisher	UOR	3
5	create_user	UOR	3
6	delete_customer	ABS—UOI	4
7	delete_publisher	ABS—UOI	4
8	delete_user	ABS—UOI	4
9	find_book_by_isbn	ABS—ROR—UOI—UOR	14
10	find_category_by_name	ABS—ROR—UOI—UOR	14
11	find_customer_by_name	ABS—ROR—UOI—UOR	14
12	find_publisher_by_name	ABS—ROR—UOI—UOR	14
13	find_user_by_username	ABS—ROR—UOI—UOR	14
14	purchase_book	ABS—AOR—UOI—UOR	11
15	rent_book	ABS—AOR—UOI—UOR	11
16	return_book	ABS—AOR—UOI—UOR	11
17	update_user_password	ABS—UOI	4
Total			134

10.6 Limitations and Assumptions

Due to the limitations of the Spec# constructs and the Boogie tool verification capabilities, we have applied some simplifications on our model to facilitate its implementation. In this section, we explain these simplifications and show that the simplified implementation is operationally equivalent to a one that would employ our proposed model.

As an example, we consider modeling a Book table used by the Book Rental application. A Book is described in the database by an ISBN, title, author, publisher, category and a quantity as shown in Fig. 10.2.

A couple of sample records are shown in Fig. 10.3. Our proposed model represents the Book table as a set of Book records. Using this set-based model, the book data can be represented as the set of two book records marked in Fig. 10.3a as records A and B. However, the Boogie verifier used in our experiment fails to prove some of the assertions for user-defined objects. To overcome this limitation, we employ arrays, instead of sets, to represent our data structure as the tool has better

Book	
Field Name	**Data Type**
ISBN	Text
Title	Text
Author	Text
Publisher	Text
Category	Text
Quantity	Number

Fig. 10.2 The Book database table design

a

	ISBN	Title	Author	Publisher	Category	Quantity
Record A	0142000280	Getting Things Done	David Allen	Penguin	non-fiction	1
Record B	0545162076	Harry Potter	Joanne Kathleen	Arthur Levine	fiction	2
*						

The set-based representation of the book data

b

	isbns	titles	authors	publishers	categories	quantities
	ISBN	Title	Author	Publisher	Category	Quantity
	0142000280	Getting Things Done	David Allen	Penguin	non-fiction	1
	0545162076	Harry Potter	Joanne Kathleen	Arthur Levine	fiction	2
pointer → *						

The array-based representation of the book data

Fig. 10.3 A graphical representation of the Book data model. (**a**) The set-based representation of the book data. (**b**) The array-based representation of the book data

``class BookRentalDataModel
{

  Set<BookRecord> books;
  …
}

class BookRecord
  {
    int key;
    string isbn;
    string title;
    string author;
    string publisher;
    string category;
    int quantity;
  }
``` | ```class BookRentalDataModel
  {
    int[] book_isbns;
    int[] book_titles;
    int[] book_authors;
    int[] book_publishers;
    int[] book_categories;
    int[] book_quantities;

    int book_pointer;
    …
  }
``` |
| (a) The Book data model class | (b) The simplified Book data model class |

Listing 10.1 The set-based and array-based implementations of the Book model

support for reasoning about arrays. Using arrays, the same data can alternatively be represented with six arrays as shown Fig. 10.3b. A pointer is used to keep track of the first empty position in an array for element insertion.

We also avoid non-simple data types such as strings and represent the data using positive integers (the value −1 is reserved to denote a deleted value). Since our reasoning tasks focus on specifying data changes, the data types are irrelevant in our case. Listing 10.1a is the set-based implementation of the Book model and Listing 10.1b is the corresponding array-based implementation.

Next, Listing 10.2a show the specification of the CRUD operations for the Book model, using the set-based modeling and Listing 10.2b show the corresponding array-based implementation and specification. As can be seen in Listing 10.2b, we provide the implementation of each of the CRUD operations as the Boogie verifier does not support the specification of abstract methods. The implementation is required by the verifier to reason about the side effects of each operation.

10.7   Results and Analysis

10.7.1   Mutation Score

For each method used in our experiment, we calculated the mutation score at different levels of specifications. We then analyzed the results to test if there's a significant difference achieved at the different specification levels. The results are represented using the boxplot in Fig. 10.4. The difference in code properties among the different methods result in the skewness of the results observed at partial specification levels. For example, some methods, like *delete_user,* don't have loops in the

```
// Finding a record using a record's key
[Pure] public abstract BookRecord findRecordByKey(int key)
ensures (exists{BookRecord rec; this.books.Contains(rec) && rec.key == key
&& result == rec)) || (result == null);

// Finding a record by a criteria, the ISBN is an example
[Pure] public abstract BookRecord findRecordByISBN(string isbn)
ensures (exists{int j in (0:this.books.Length-1); this.books[j]==(result)
&& this.books[j].isbn == isbn }) || (result == null);

// Creating a record
[Pure] public abstract BookRentalDataModel createRecord(BookRecord rec)
ensures result.books == this.books.Union(rec);

// Deleting a record
[Pure] public abstract BookRentalDataModel deleteRecord(int key)
ensures result.books == this.books.Difference(findRecordByKey(key))

// Updating a record
[Pure] public abstract BookRentalDataModel updateRecord(BookRecord newRec)
ensures result == this.deleteRecord(newRec.key).createRecord(newRec)
```

          (a)   The specification of the CRUD operations

```
// Helper method
[Pure] public bool isBooksFull()
ensures result == (book_pointer == book_isbns.Length);
{
  return (book_pointer == book_isbns.Length);
}

// Finding a record using a record's key
[Pure] public int findRecordByKey(int key)
ensures 0 <= result ==> book_isbns[result] != -1 && result == key;
ensures result < 0 --> result != key;
ensures result < book_pointer;
{
  if(key < book_pointer) && book_isbns[key]!= -1) return key;
  else return -1;
}

// Finding a record by a criteria, the ISBN is an example
[Pure] public int findRecordByISBN(int isbn)
ensures 0 <= result ==> book_isbns[result] == isbn;
ensures result < book_pointer;
{
  int n = book_pointer;
  do {
    n--;
    if (n < 0)
      {
        break;
      }
  } while (book_isbns[n] != isbn);
```

Listing 10.2 The implementation and specification of the Book model operations

```
    return n;
}

// Creating a record
public void createRecord(int isbn, int title, int author, int publisher,
int quantity, int category)
requires !isBooksFull();
requires find_author(author) >= 0;
requires find_publisher(publisher) >= 0;
requires find_category(quantity) >= 0;
ensures book_isbns[old(book_pointer)] == isbn;
ensures book_titles[old(book_pointer)] == title;
ensures book_authors[old(book_pointer)] == author;
ensures book_publishers[old(book_pointer)] == publisher;
ensures book_categories[old(book_pointer)] == category;
ensures book_quantities[old(book_pointer)] == quantity;
ensures book_pointer == old(book_pointer) + 1;
ensures exists{int x in (0: book_isbns.Length); book_isbns[x] == isbn &&
book_titles[x] == title && book_authors[x] == author && book_publishers[x]
== publisher && book_categories[x] == category && book_quantities[x] ==
quantity};
{
    book_isbns[book_pointer] = isbn;
    book_titles[book_pointer] = title;
    book_authors[book_pointer] = author;
    book_publishers[book_pointer] = publisher;
    book_categories[book_pointer] = category;
    book_quantities[book_pointer] = quantity;
    book_pointer++;
}

// Deleting a record
public void deleteRecord (int key)
requires findRecordByKey(key) >=0;
ensures book_isbns[key] == -1;
ensures book_titles[key] == -1;
ensures book_authors[key] == -1;
ensures book_publishers[key] == -1;
ensures book_categories [key] == -1;
ensures book_quantities[key] == -1;
{
    book_isbns[key] = -1;
    book_titles[key] = -1;
    book_authors[key] = -1;
    book_publishers[key] = -1;
    book_categories[key] = -1;
    book_quantities[key] = -1;
}

// Updating a record
public void updateRecord (int key, int newIsbn, int newTitle, int
newAuthor, int newPublisher, int newCategory, int newQuantity)
requires findRecordByKey(key) >=0;
ensures book_isbns[key] == newIsbn;
ensures book_titles[key] == newTitle;
ensures book_authors[key] == newAuthor;
```

Listing 10.2 (continued)

```
ensures book_publishers[key] == newPublisher;
ensures book_categories [key] == newCategory;
ensures book_quantities[key] == newQuantity;
ensures exists{int x in (0: book_isbns.Length); book_isbns[x] == newIsbn
&& book_titles[x] == newTitle && book_authors[x] == newAuthor &&
book_publishers[x] == newPublisher && book_categories[x] == newCategory &&
book_quantities[x] == newQuantity};
{
  book_isbns[key] = newIsbn;
  book_titles[key] = newTitle;
  book_authors[key] = newAuthor;
  book_publishers[key] = newPublisher;
  book_categories [key] = newCategory;
  book_quantities[key] = newQuantity;
}
```

(b) The implementation and specification of the array-based CRUD
operations

Listing 10.2 (continued)

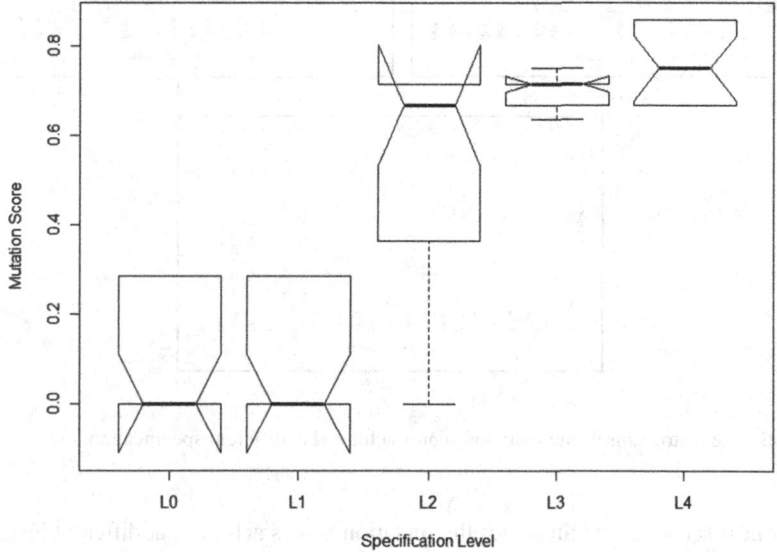

Fig. 10.4 The mutation scores achieved at different specification levels

code and hence the specification doesn't include invariants. Consequently, adding loop invariants at L2 has no effect on the mutation score. At L4, each method is specified with one or more specification construct which leads to a more symmetric distribution as shown in the boxplot.

It should be noted here that the mutation tool generates errors that are syntactically correct and hence none of these injected errors are detected by the C# non-verifying compiler. In other words, the mutation score of the non-verifying compiler is consistently equal to zero.

Figure 10.5 shows the histogram of the mutation score, as percentage, achieved at the different levels.

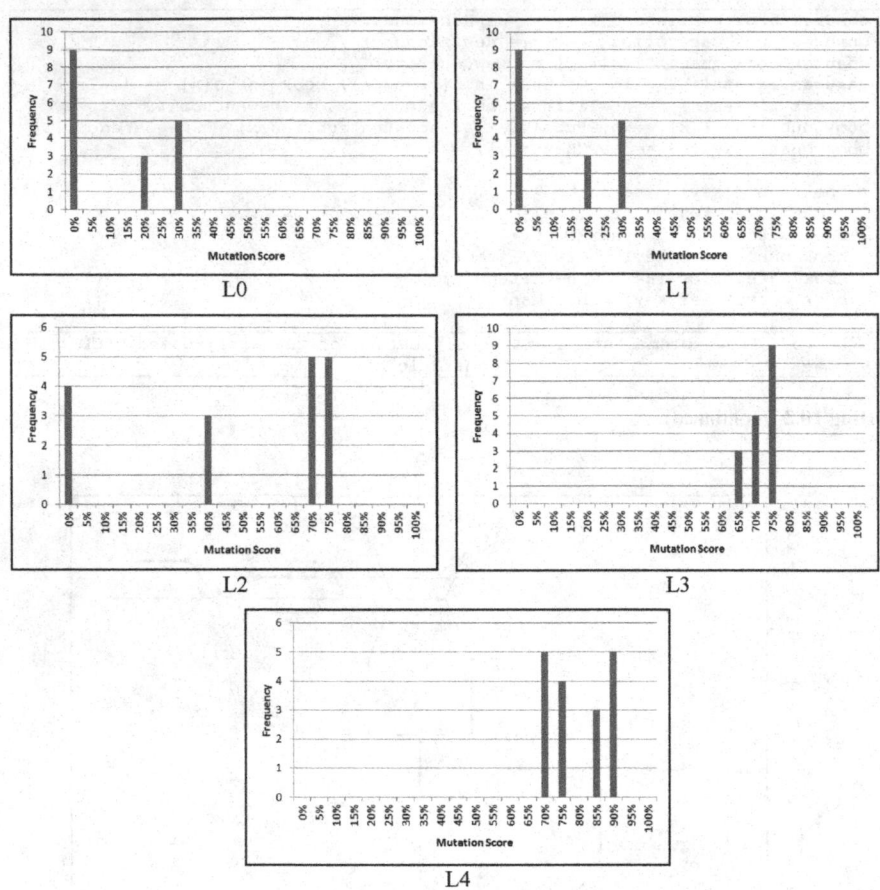

Fig. 10.5 The histograms of the mutation scores achieved at different specification levels

Our next set of results illustrates the mutation scores achieved at different levels of specifications for different types of mutation errors. The results are depicted in Fig. 10.6.

As seen in the figure, L4 performs the best by detecting the highest number of errors across different error types while L3 comes at the second rank. The difference of mutation score achieved by these two levels is not significant though which implies that there isn't a large benefit in adding postconditions. This is however due to the fact that postconditions used in the experiment could not be exhaustive due to verifier limitations. We will elaborate on these limitations later with examples.

There's no significant difference between L0 and L1 and they both perform significantly worse than the other levels. The mutation scores achieved by L2 are higher, however, the high variance of L2 results comes from the fact that L2 performance depend heavily on the type of mutation. In the following subsection, we take a closer look on the results with some of the examples where errors are not detected by the specification.

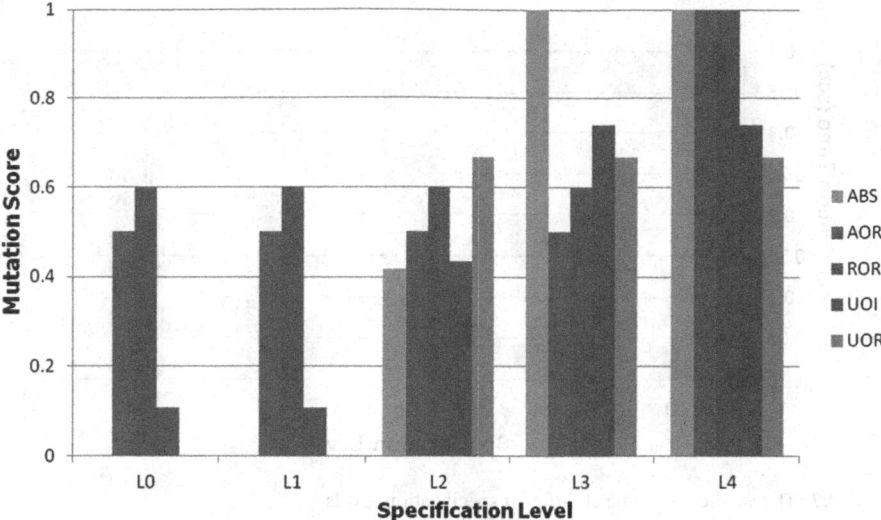

Fig. 10.6 The mutation scores achieved at different specification levels for different types of mutation operators

10.7.2 Observations

As shown in the results, some mutations are not killed by any of the specification levels. By investigating these mutations, it turned out that they actually do not introduce a logical error but only affect code readability or performance. For example, in C#, the prefix and postfix notations of the increment/decrement operator differ only in the returned value but both affect a variable in the same way. Consequently, a UOR error that replaces ––n to n–– does not introduce an error as long as the statement's return value is not used in the code. Similarly, an UOI error that replaces int n=category_pointer with int n=+category_pointer only affects code readability, since category_pointer is defined as non-negative integer with the invariant 0 <= category_pointer. These errors do not introduce a logical error, and hence they are not signaled by the verifier as a contract violation. In the experiment, this was the case with the 25 mutations that are not detected by the highest level of specifications. Another observation is that invariants' role in detecting errors depends on the error type and hence the variance of the results at L2.

10.7.3 Verification Time

In this section, we present some performance analysis of the verification process. The goal is to show the feasibility of using a verifying-compiler. The verification times are calculated by running the Boogie verifier on Spec# programs on an Intel Core i3 CPU, 2.13 GHz machine with 8 GB RAM and 64-bit operating system.

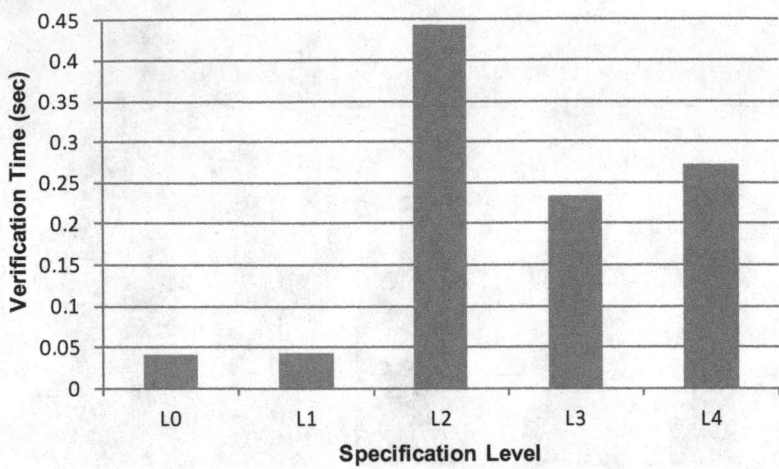

Fig. 10.7 The verification time at different specification levels

Figure 10.7 shows the verification time for each of the five verification levels. As seen from the results, L2 is the most expensive in terms of verification time. It's interesting to note that adding more specifications at L3 and L4 decreases the verification time needed to prove the code correctness as more help is given to the static checker.

10.7.4   Validity Discussion

In this section, we discuss some threats to our experiment both from internal and external validity standpoints. Some of the threats are very similar to the ones we described in the previous chapter.

10.7.4.1   Internal Validity

First, we used in our experiment a mutation tool implemented by the authors of [89, 92]. The types of mutations introduced by the tool depend on the code and hence not all mutation types can be tested.

10.7.4.2   External Validity

We have used C# and Spec# as our programming and specification languages, respectively. Hence, care should be taken if results are to be generalized to other languages, especially if different verification techniques are used.

10.8 Conclusions

The experiment described in this chapter empirically illustrates that adding our formal model and contracts to data-centric services' code can enable the detection of programmer's errors at design-time. We have shown by using statistical methods that the higher the level of specification, the higher the probability of detecting errors. Based on our results, we can sort the specification levels by their ability of detecting errors in the code (results regarding invariants are indecisive due to the high variance in the mutation score):

1. The highest level of specifications
2. Preconditions
3. Invariants
4. Non-null types or no specification

The highest level of specification enabled detection of *all* valid errors. Errors not detected by that level were errors that only affect code readability and not its correctness.

Chapter 11
Design-by-Contract for Web Services

Abstract Unlike software components operating within an enterprise, the Web services model establishes a loosely coupled relationship between a service producer and a service consumer. Service consumers have little control over services that they employ within their applications. A service is hosted on its provider's server and is invoked remotely by a consumer over the Web. In such settings, it is important to establish a contract between the service provider and the service consumer. The contract establishes a set of obligations and expectations. These obligations can be functional, specifying the service operations in terms of its pre/postconditions. They can also be non-functional pertaining to legal, security, availability and performance aspects.

Applying design-by-contract principles in the context of Web services addresses many practical challenges. From the perspective of a service producer, a Web service must be designed and implemented to be broadly applicable. Quoting [32], "[The concept of broad applicability] suggests that the eventual uses of any given service can't be predicted at the time the service is created... In other words: Design and implement your Web service interfaces to handle anything that might be thrown at them". Accordingly, the service implementation must cover all possible invocation scenarios. This can be done by adding defensive checks to the service implementation. However, while these checks may ensure that the service is invoked with the correct input, they can affect the code efficiency in a negative way. The authors of [98] present a relevant example; consider a binary search method that requires its array argument to be sorted. Checking that an array is sorted requires time linear in the length of the array, but the binary search routine is supposed to execute in a logarithmic time. Design-by-contract techniques help avoiding these inefficient checks by explicitly adding pre-conditions on the service inputs. It is then the consumer's responsibility to satisfy these pre-conditions in order to guarantee that the service behaves as expected. Moreover, if these pre-conditions are formally defined, then the consumer can use automatic reasoning tools to check his/her implementation and to guarantee that it satisfies the pre-conditions.

From a consumer perspective, the integration of a Web service into an online application involves several risks; How to guarantee that future service updates will not break the application? How to guarantee that a service request does not generate an error? More important, how to guarantee that the service does not act in a way

© Springer International Publishing Switzerland 2015   109
I. Saleh, *Formalizing Data-Centric Web Services*, Web-Scale Workflow
and Analytics, DOI 10.1007/978-3-319-24678-9_11

that is not intended by the service consumer even if it does not return an error? This is where the formal contract comes into play by exposing some obligations that the service provider has to maintain by the underlying implementation. The service provider can make updates to the service implementation as long as these updates do not violate the exposed contract. Additionally, a formal contract would enable the service consumer to use automatic reasoning tools to check that the updated implementation still complies with the contract. The contract would also ensure that, whenever the service pre-conditions are met, the service is guaranteed to have the result and side-effect specified by the post-conditions. The consumer can hence effectively identify erroneous inputs, and invocations that may not produce the intended results or side-effects.

From a practicality standpoint, it is unrealistic to assume that service providers will fully specify all their services. For this reason, we show in this book how our model can support both lightweight and heavyweight specification. Moreover, our evaluation of the Amazon.com *ItemSearch* data contract demonstrates how the contract, at different level of sophistication, can be very useful in making the interaction with a service more efficient and effective. The Web crawling case study that we use shows how even a partial contract can significantly disambiguate the service behavior. The e-commerce scenario presents another case study where a lightweight specification can be used to prove that data integrity properties are maintained by a transaction design. Such proofs are of great importance especially when the transaction involves transferring funds between financial accounts, as demonstrated in our example.

Recently, there have been efforts for integrating formal specification techniques into mainstream programming languages. The Java Modeling Language (JML) [26] for Java and the Spec# language [17] for C# are two examples. Both languages use constructs with similar syntax to the programming language that they specify. The advantage of using these languages in writing the contract is that it is easier for programmers to learn and less intimidating than languages that use special-purpose mathematical notations [98].

While the Web service reuse model imposes a number of challenges, there is also a number of interesting opportunities that arise from that same model. Unlike many reusable components, Web Services are executed at the provider's end. Consequently, service providers can monitor the invocation of their services and collect valuable information about reuse patterns and invocation errors. Capturing user errors while invoking services help service providers empirically evaluate the quality of the specifications. By using these errors as feedback, the formal contract of a service can be continuously enhanced throughout its lifetime.

Another interesting opportunity is the empowerment of the online community. A successful service is an online asset that attracts a large number of developers. Amazon.com for example claims that more than a million customers are using their e-commerce services as of January 2015 [99]. The service providers typically have online forums where these developers share their experience, report bugs and request others' help with service usage. Alternatively, service providers can leverage the power of this community to collaboratively build services' contracts. Contracts can be built and modified based on the consumer's experience and by formalizing online documentation. This is similar to our approach in building the Web services data models and contracts presented in this book.

Chapter 12
Summary and Conclusions

Abstract In this work, we show how formal contracts can facilitate the specification and verification of data centric Web services. Our work comes to fill a practical gap in current Web services' specification techniques; the specification of the data logic and related business rules is overlooked. We show how this gap currently contributes in many problems related to the practical use of services on the Web.

While the Web service reuse model imposes a number of challenges, there is also a number of interesting opportunities that arise from that same model. Unlike many reusable components, Web Services are executed at the provider's end. Consequently, service providers can monitor the invocation of their services and collect valuable information about reuse patterns and erroneous invocation. Capturing user errors while invoking services can help service providers empirically evaluate the quality of the specifications. By using these errors as feedback, they can enhance the formal contract of a service throughout its lifetime.

Another interesting opportunity is the empowerment of the online community. A successful service is an online asset that attracts a large number of developers. Amazon.com for example claims that more than a million customers are using their e-commerce services as of January 2015 [99]. The service providers typically have online forums where these developers share their experience, report bugs and request others help with service usage. Alternatively, service providers can leverage the power of this community to collaboratively build services' contracts. Contracts can be built and modified based on the consumer's experience and by formalizing online documentation. This is similar to our approach in building the Web services data models and contracts presented in this work.

Throughout this book, we make the case, using real-life examples, that formal methods can significantly decrease ambiguity about a service behavior and can be used to verify the outcome of a composition of services. We also show how formal contracts can be useful in providing data integrity guarantees within a Web transaction and enabling the detection of errors in service-based implementations. We hence provide Web service developers and consumers with valuable tools and guidelines that enable verifying correctness of their Web service-based applications. Our approach has a sound formal foundation which opens the opportunities of many automated applications that exploit the exposed specification in order to deduce facts about service behavior.

© Springer International Publishing Switzerland 2015   111
I. Saleh, *Formalizing Data-Centric Web Services*, Web-Scale Workflow
and Analytics, DOI 10.1007/978-3-319-24678-9_12

Our empirical evaluations demonstrate how the contract, at different level of sophistication, can be very useful in making the interaction with a service more efficient and effective. We have shown by using statistical methods that the higher the level of specification, the higher the probability of detecting errors. Some errors are detected however with partial specifications.

We also present our effort in implementing our data model and contracting framework for Web services using state-of-the-art specification languages. Our experiment shows some limitations in current languages and formal verification techniques. However, we are able to verify some of the correctness properties using the current tools. While the current verification tools are not well suited yet for general and complex programs, there has been a significant progress in this area. Some recent efforts aim at integrating specification techniques into current mainstream programming languages, the C# contracts are an example. While they still lack the necessary constructs for defining abstract data types and tools for verifying complex assertions, they are however useful in detecting some logical errors in the code and enhancing automatic testing [85].

As noted in [100], there are scalability limitations related to using formal methods. Systems for reasoning with pre- and postconditions, such as Hoare axioms, have small-size atomic units and fail to scale up because they do not provide structuring or encapsulation [101]. With the current state of the formal specification languages and tools, it is still not possible to fully specify and verify every property of a large-scale system with respect to the requirements. It is however possible to verify some properties, as it is the case with our proposed model, where we focus on specifying and verifying the data aspect of a software component.

We also propose in [102] using Big Data frameworks, such as Apache Hadoop® [103] to speed up testing of code. We believe that this direction opens the door for leveraging new cloud-based systems to scale up the otherwise time-consuming code verification process.

A study of the overhead of specifying code, in terms of development effort would be a valuable addition to the current study as it would enable developers to evaluate the cost of formally specifying code versus developing testing tools. It would also facilitate a cost-benefit analysis to decide on the time and effort invested by developers in specifying their classes and the optimal type of specification used based on the characteristics of programs being developed and the developers' familiarity with the specification language and its constructs. Another interesting experiment would be to have developers implement each algorithm, introducing a larger variety of errors into the code. Such an experiment would have however to guard against some potential threats to validity, as results would largely depend on the population selected, their familiarity with the code specification practices and their level of expertise with the programming languages.

Finally, our proposed data specification can be used to enable automatic test case generations for database applications. Testing database applications involves the challenge of generating interesting database states. To comprehensively cover a database application using test cases, tests should not only provide inputs to the application itself, but also prepare necessary states in its database back-end [104]. Our general proposed solution for this problem is depicted in Fig. 12.1. As shown in the

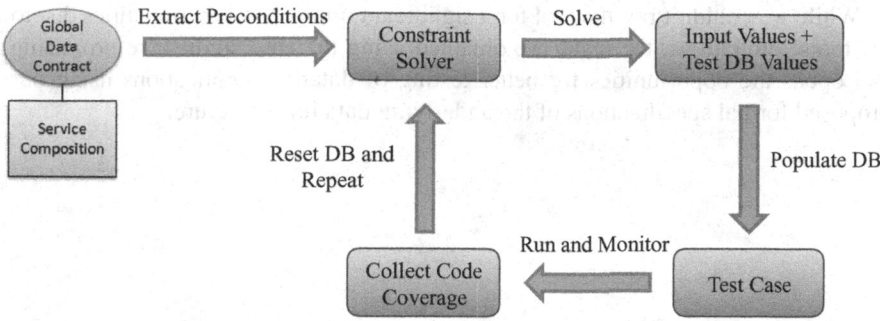

Fig. 12.1 Test case generation from formal specifications

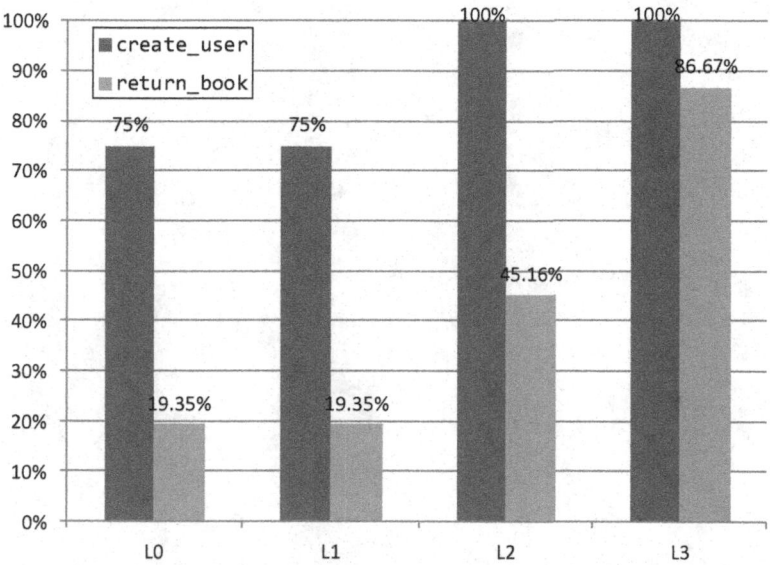

Fig. 12.2 Code coverage at different levels of specifications

figure, the service specifications are fed into a constraint solver that uses the specification to generate interesting input values. We inject our database model as an additional input to the service under test. By injecting the database model as an input parameter, the constraint solver can generate test values for the database as well. These test values are used to populate the database before running the unit tests.

Our experimentation with two case studies show that better unit tests, with higher code coverage, can be generated by adding the database model as a variable, in a database application, and specifying the data logic using our contracting framework. Some exploratory results are depicted in Fig. 12.2 for specifying two services in the book rental application described earlier in this book.

While we couldn't run the tool for a significant number of functionalities due to the tools' limitations, the result we obtained using the case studies are promising and opens the opportunities for better testing of database applications using our proposed formal specifications of the underlying data infrastructure.

Chapter 13
Appendix A: The Amazon Item Search
Implementation in JML

This appendix contains the Java Modeling Language (JML) version of ItemSeach data model and data contract presented in the book. JML annotations are appended to java code as comments proceeded by the at-sign (@). JML uses a requires clause to specify the client's obligation (pre-conditions) and an ensures clause to specify the implementer's obligation (post-conditions). The \result variable denotes the output of a method. A complete reference of the JML syntax can be found in [62].

© Springer International Publishing Switzerland 2015
I. Saleh, *Formalizing Data-Centric Web Services*, Web-Scale Workflow
and Analytics, DOI 10.1007/978-3-319-24678-9_13

```
1   package aws;
2
3   import org.jmlspecs.models.JMLEqualsSet;
4
5   public abstract class ItemSearchDataModel {
6
7   //@ public instance invariant
8   //@ (\forall Object c; this.itemEntity.has(c); c instanceof
    ItemRecord);
9
10  /*@ spec_public @*/JMLEqualsSet itemEntity;
11
12  //@ ensures  (\result.key  ==  key  &&  this.itemEntity.has
    (\result))|| \result == null;
13  public/*@pure*/ abstract ItemRecord findRecordByKey(Integer
    key);
14
15  /*@ //@ ensures this.itemEntity.has(\result);
16   @ ensures !authors.isEmpty() ==>
17   @ (\forall ItemRecord r; \result.has(r);
18   @ r instanceof ItemRecord && authors.has(r.author));
19   @
20   @ ensures !artists.isEmpty() ==>
21   @ (\forall ItemRecord r; \result.has(r);
22   @ r instanceof ItemRecord && artists.has(r.artist));
23   @
24   @ ensures (* similar assertions for titles, categories,  *);
25  */
26  public  /*@pure*/abstract  JMLEqualsSet  findRecordByCriteria
    (JMLEqualsSet authors,
27  JMLEqualsSet  artists,  JMLEqualsSet  titles,  JMLEqualsSet
    categories,JMLEqualsSet
28  merchantNames,      JMLEqualsSet     prices,      JMLEqualsSet
    stockLevels);
29
30  //@ requires this.findRecordByKey(rec.key) == null;
31  //@ ensures
32  //@ (\forall ItemRecord r; \result.itemEntity.has(r); this.
    itemEntity.has(r));
33  //@ ensures \result.itemEntity.has(rec);
34  public /*@pure*/abstract ItemSearchDataModel createRecord
    ( ItemRecord rec);
35
36  //@ requires this.findRecordByKey(key) != null;
37  //@ ensures (\forall ItemRecord r; this.itemEntity.has(r) &&
    r.key != key;
```

```
38  \result.itemEntity.has(r));
39  public /*@pure*/abstract ItemSearchDataModel deleteRecord
    (Integer key);
40
41  //@ requires this.findRecordByKey(rec.key) != null;
42  //@  ensures  \result  ==  this.deleteRecord(rec.key).
    createRecord(rec);
43  public /*@pure*/abstract ItemSearchDataModel updateRecord(
    ItemRecord rec);
44  }
45
46  public abstract class ItemRecord {
47  /*@ spec_public @*/ protected int key;
48  /*@ spec_public @*/ protected String category;
49  /*@ spec_public @*/ protected String merchantName, title;
50  /*@ spec_public @*/ protected String author, artist;
51  /*@ spec_public @*/ protected double price;
52  /*@ spec_public @*/ protected int stockLevel;
53  /*@ public invariant (category =="CD"||category == "DVD")
54    @ ==> author == null;
55    @ public invariant (category == "Book")
56    @ ==> artist == null;
57    @ public invariant price >= 0.0;
58    @ public invariant stockLevel >= 0;
59    @ public invariant merchantName != null;
60    @ public invariant title != null;
61  */
62  }
```

The data model is used to write the contract for the Amazon ItemSearch service as follows:

```
1   /*@ public model instance non_null JMLEqualsSet categories,
    authors, artists, titles,merchantNames,
2     @ searchIndices, prices, stockLevels;
3     @ public model instance non_null ItemSearchDataModel isdm;
4     @ requires minPrice.doubleValue() >= 0.0 && maxPrice.dou-
    bleValue() >= 0.0 && minPrice <= maxPrice;
5     @ ensures \result.length >= 0; */
6   // Specifying the results in terms of the service inputs and
    the defined model
7   /*@ ensures (\forall ItemRecord r; ;(\exists int i; 0 <= i
    && i < \result.length;
8     @ isdm.findRecordByCriteria(authors, artists, titles, cat-
    egories, merchantNames, prices, stockLevels).has(r) <==>
```

```
9    @ \result[i].itemId == r.key && \result[i].detailPageURL
     == "http://www.amazon.com"+r.key
10   @ && \result[i].title == r.title && \result[i].author ==
     r.author && \result[i].artist == r.artist)); */
11   // Case 1: searching by keywords in the CD and DVD categories
12   /*@ ensures (#keywords != null) && (#searchIndex == "CD"
     || #searchIndex != "DVD") ==>
13   @searchIndices.has("DVD")   &&   searchIndices.has("CD")&&
     artists.has(#keywords) && titles.has(#keywords);*/
14   // Case 2: searching by keywords in the Books category
15   /*@ ensures #keywords != null) && (#searchIndex == "Books") ==>
16   @searchIndices.has("Book")   &&   searchIndices.has("CD")&&
     authors.has(#keywords) && titles.has(#keywords);*/
17   // Case 3: searching by keywords in all categories of items
18   /*@ ensures (#keywords != null) && (#searchIndex == "All") ==>
19   @searchIndices.has("Book") && searchIndices.has("CD")  &&
     searchIndices.has("Book") && titles.has(#keywords); */
20   // Case 4: searching by title in the Books category
21   /*@ ensures (#title != null) && (#searchIndex == "Books") ==>
22   @ searchIndices.has("Book") && titles.has(#title); */
23   // Case 5: searching by author in the Books category
24   /*@ ensures (#author != null) && (#searchIndex == "Books") ==>
25   @searchIndices.has("Book") && authors.has(#author);*/
26   // Filtering results by the min and max prices
27   /*@ ensures (#minPrice != null) ==>
28   @ (!prices.isEmpty() && (\forall Double d; prices.has(d);
     d.doubleValue()- #minPrice.doubleValue() >= 0.0));
29   @ ensures (#maxPrice != null) ==>
30   @ (!prices.isEmpty() && (\forall Double d; prices.has(d);
     #maxPrice.doubleValue())- d.doubleValue() >= 0.0))*/
31   // Filtering results by availability
32   /*@ ensures (#availability == "Available") ==>
33   @ (!stockLevels.isEmpty() && (\forall Integer i; stockLev-
     els.has(i); i.intValue() > 0));
34   @ ensures (#availability == null) ==>
35   @ (!stockLevels.isEmpty() && (\forall Integer i; stockLevels.
     has(i); i.intValue() >=0));*/
36   // Filtering results by the merchant name, this parameter has
     a default value "Amazon"
37   /*@ ensures  (#merchant  !=  null)  ==>  merchantNames.
     has(#merchant);
38   @ ensures (#merchant == null)==> merchantNames.has("Amazon"); */
39   // Results are sorted based on the value of the sort input
40   /*@ ensures (#sort == "price") ==>
```

```
41    @(\forall int i;0 <= i && i < \result.length-1; \result[i+1].
      price.doubleValue()-\result[i].price.doubleValue()>=0.0);
42    @ ensures (#sort == "-price") ==>
43    @(\forall int i;0 <= i && i < \result.length-1;\result[i].
      price.doubleValue()-\result[i+1].price.doubleValue()>=
      0.0);*/
```

Chapter 14
Appendix B: A Prolog Reasoner

The following code is for a reasoner in Prolog that implements the Amazon ItemSearch service assertions and the Web crawling logic described in Chap. 8. The reasoner produces the total number of possible queries the Web crawler has to try against the Web service given the service specifications. A sample output is provided.

© Springer International Publishing Switzerland 2015
I. Saleh, *Formalizing Data-Centric Web Services*, Web-Scale Workflow
and Analytics, DOI 10.1007/978-3-319-24678-9_14

```
:- use_module(library(clpfd)).
:- use_module(library(simplex)).
:- use_module(library(lists)).
```

% A list maximum predicate that can get the maximum with the
existance of sublists within the given list

```
max([], MaxSoFar, MaxSoFar).

max([Number|Rest], MaxSoFar, Max) :-
       is_list(Number),
       max(Number, MaxSoFar, SubMax),!,
       max([SubMax| Rest], MaxSoFar, Max).

max([Number|Rest], MaxSoFar, Max) :-
       Number > MaxSoFar,
       max(Rest, Number, Max).

max([Number|Rest], MaxSoFar, Max) :-
       Number =< MaxSoFar,
       max(Rest, MaxSoFar, Max).
```
% The ItemSearch Service Specification levels

% Level 0: no specification
```
itemSearchL0(SearchIndex, Title, Author, Artist, Keywords,
MinPrice, MaxPrice, Merchant, Availability, Sort) :-
CD = 1, DVD = 2, Book = 3, All = 4, SearchIndex in (CD \/ DVD \/
Book \/ All),
Null = 0, Minvalue = 1, Maxvalue =2, MinPrice in (Null \/
Minvalue \/ Maxvalue),
MaxPrice in (Null \/ Minvalue \/ Maxvalue),
Avail = 1, Asc = 1, Desc = 2,
St1 = 1, St2 = 2, Title in (St1 \/ St2 \/ Null), Author in (St1
\/ St2 \/ Null),
Artist in (St1 \/ St2 \/ Null), Keywords in (St1 \/ St2 \/ Null),
Merchant in (St1 \/ St2 \/ Null), Availability in (Avail \/
Null), Sort in (Asc \/ Desc).
```

% Get Number if Possible input combinations given level 0
service specification
```
demonstrateL0 :- nl,
               write('L0; No Specification Case\n'),
               itemSearchL0(SearchIndex, Title, Author, Artist,
Keywords, MinPrice, MaxPrice, Merchant, Availability, Sort),
               findall([SearchIndex, Title, Author, Artist, Keywords,
MinPrice, MaxPrice, Merchant, Availability, Sort],
               label([SearchIndex, Title, Author, Artist, Keywords,
MinPrice, MaxPrice, Merchant, Availability, Sort]), N),
               length(N,Sol), write('Total Number of Possible Service
Queries: '), write(Sol).
```

```
% Level 1 specification
itemSearchL1(SearchIndex,  Title,  Author,  Artist,  Keywords,
MinPrice, MaxPrice, Merchant, Availability, Sort) :-
CD = 1, DVD = 2, Book = 3, All = 4, SearchIndex in (CD \/ DVD \/
Book \/ All),
  Null = 0, Minvalue = 1, Maxvalue =2, MinPrice in (Null \/
Minvalue \/ Maxvalue),
    MaxPrice in (Null \/ Minvalue \/ Maxvalue),
    Avail = 1, Asc = 1, Desc = 2,
  (MinPrice #=< MaxPrice) #\/ (MinPrice #= Null) #\/ (MaxPrice #=Null),
    St1 = 1, St2 = 2, Title in (St1 \/ St2 \/ Null), Author in (St1
\/ St2 \/ Null),
    Artist in (St1 \/ St2 \/ Null), Keywords in (St1 \/ St2 \/ Null),
      Merchant in (St1 \/ St2 \/ Null), Availability in (Avail \/
Null), Sort in (Asc \/ Desc).

% Get Number if Possible input combinations given level 1 ser-
vice specification
  demonstrateL1 :- nl,
              write('Level 1 Specification Case\n'),
              itemSearchL1(SearchIndex, Title, Author, Artist,
    Keywords, MinPrice, MaxPrice, Merchant, Availability, Sort),
              findall([SearchIndex, Title, Author, Artist, Keywords,
    MinPrice, MaxPrice, Merchant, Availability, Sort],
              label([SearchIndex, Title, Author, Artist, Keywords,
    MinPrice, MaxPrice, Merchant, Availability, Sort]), N),
              length(N,Sol),  write('Total  Number  of  Possible
              Service
    Queries: '), write(Sol).

% Level 2 Service Specification
% Level 2 is described using three different predicates to cover
three search cases
% 1] search in either CD, DVD categories
  itemSearchL2(SearchIndex,  Title,  Author,  Artist,  Keywords,
MinPrice, MaxPrice, Merchant, Availability, Sort, SearchIndex_Set) :-
          CD = 1, DVD = 2, SearchIndex in (CD \/ DVD),
          Null = 0, Minvalue = 1, Maxvalue =2, MinPrice in (Null \/
      Minvalue \/ Maxvalue),
          MaxPrice in (Null \/ Minvalue \/ Maxvalue),
          Avail = 1, Asc = 1, Desc = 2,
          (MinPrice  #=<  MaxPrice)  #\/  (MinPrice  #=  Null)  #\/
      (MaxPrice #=Null),
          St1 = 1, St2 = 2, Title in (St1 \/ St2 \/ Null), Author = Null,
          Artist in (St1 \/ St2 \/ Null), Keywords in (St1 \/ St2 \/
      Null),
```

```
        Merchant in (St1 \/ St2 \/ Null), Availability in (Avail
    \/ Null), Sort in (Asc \/ Desc),
        SearchIndex_Set = 1.


  % 2] Search in Book category
   itemSearchL2(SearchIndex,  Title,  Author,  Artist,  Keywords,
MinPrice, MaxPrice, Merchant, Availability, Sort, SearchIndex_Set) :-
        Book = 3, SearchIndex = Book,
        Null = 0, Minvalue = 1, Maxvalue =2, MinPrice in (Null \/
    Minvalue \/ Maxvalue), MaxPrice in (Null \/ Minvalue \/
    Maxvalue),
           Avail = 1, Asc = 1, Desc = 2,
           (MinPrice #=< MaxPrice) #\/ (MinPrice #= Null)
        #\/ (MaxPrice #=Null),
           St1 = 1, St2 = 2, Title in (St1 \/ St2 \/ Null),
        Artist = Null,
           Author in (St1 \/ St2 \/ Null), Keywords in (St1
        \/ St2 \/ Null),
           Merchant in (St1 \/ St2 \/ Null), Availability in
        (Avail \/ Null), Sort in (Asc \/ Desc),
           SearchIndex_Set = 1.


  % 3] Search in All items by keywords
   itemSearchL2(SearchIndex,  Title,  Author,  Artist,  Keywords,
MinPrice, MaxPrice, Merchant, Availability, Sort, SearchIndex_Set) :-
           All = 4, SearchIndex = All,
           Null = 0, Minvalue = 1, Maxvalue =2, MinPrice in
           (Null \/ Minvalue \/ Maxvalue), MaxPrice in (Null \/
           Minvalue \/ Maxvalue),
           Avail = 1, Asc = 1, Desc = 2,
           (MinPrice #=< MaxPrice) #\/ (MinPrice #= Null)
        #\/ (MaxPrice #=Null),
           St1 = 1, St2 = 2, Title = Null, Artist = Null,
           Author = Null, Keywords in (St1 \/ St2),
           Merchant in (St1 \/ St2 \/ Null), Availability in
        (Avail \/ Null), Sort in (Asc \/ Desc),
           SearchIndex_Set = 3.
           % Get Number if Possible input combinations given
           level 1 service specification
    demonstrateL2 :- nl,
           write('Level 2 Specification Case\n'),
           itemSearchL2(SearchIndex, Title, Author, Artist,
Keywords,  MinPrice,  MaxPrice,  Merchant,  Availability,  Sort,
SearchIndex_Set),
```

```
        findall([SearchIndex, Title, Author, Artist, Keywords,
MinPrice, MaxPrice, Merchant, Availability, Sort],
        label([SearchIndex,   Title,   Author,   Artist,
Keywords, MinPrice, MaxPrice, Merchant, Availability,
Sort]), N),
        length(N,Sol), write('Total Number of Possible
Service Queries: '), write(Sol).


% Deep Web Crawler logic begins here
% Get all possible values for the SearchIndex Set.
valueSearchIndex_Set(V) :- itemSearchL2(S, T, A, Ar, K, Minp,
Maxp, Mer, Av, Srt, SI_Set),findall(SI_Set, label([SI_Set]), V).


allvalueSearchIndex_Set(Vs) :-bagof(V, valueSearchIndex_Set(V), Vs).


% Maximize the returned results by maximizing the size of the
SearchIndex Set
    selectSearchIndex_Set(SI)    :-    allvalueSearchIndex_Set(Vs),
max(Vs, -1, SI).


    solution(Queries) :- nl, write('Demonstrating different levels
of service specification'), nl,
                demonstrateL0, demonstrateL1,
                nl, write('Level 2 Specification Case '),
                s e l e c t S e a r c h I n d e x _ S e t ( S I _ S e t ) ,
                itemSearchL2(SearchIndex, Title, Author, Artist,
Keywords, MinPrice, MaxPrice, Merchant, Availability,
Sort, SI_Set),
                findall([SearchIndex,   Title,   Author,   Artist,
Keywords, MinPrice, MaxPrice, Merchant, Availability,
Sort],
                label([SearchIndex,   Title,   Author,   Artist,
Keywords, MinPrice, MaxPrice, Merchant, Availability,
Sort]), Queries),
                nl, write('Results maximized at SearchIndex='),
write(SearchIndex),
                length(Queries,Sol), nl, nl, write('Total Number
of Possible Service Queries: '),write(Sol), nl.


    ?- solution(Q).


Demonstrating different levels of service specification
L0; No Specification Case
Total Number of Possible Service Queries: 34992
```

```
        Level 1 Specification Case
        Total Number of Possible Service Queries: 31104
        Level 2 Specification Case
        Results maximized at SearchIndex=4

   Total Number of Possible Service Queries: 192
   Q = [[4, 0, 0, 0, 1, 0, 0, 0|…], [4, 0, 0, 0, 1, 0, 0|…], [4, 0,
0, 0, 1, 0|…], [4, 0, 0, 0, 1|…], [4, 0, 0, 0|…], [4, 0, 0|…], [4,
0|…], [4|…], […|…]|…] ;
   false.
```

References

1. "Web Services Description Language (WSDL) Version 2.0," 2007. [Online]. Available: http://www.w3.org/TR/wsdl20/.
2. "RESTful Web Services: The basics." [Online]. Available: http://www.ibm.com/developer-works/library/ws-restful/.
3. "Web Application Description Language (WADL)." [Online]. Available: https://wadl.java.net/.
4. "Business Process Execution Language for Web Services version 1.1," 08-Feb-2007. [Online]. Available: http://www.ibm.com/developerworks/library/specification/ws-bpel/.
5. "OWL-S: Semantic Markup for Web Services," 2004. [Online]. Available: http://www.w3.org/Submission/2004/SUBM-OWL-S-20041122/.
6. "Amazon," *Amzaon Online Shopping Site*. [Online]. Available: http://www.amazon.com/.
7. "PayPal Electronic Payment Site." [Online]. Available: https://www.paypal.com.
8. "FedEx Shipping Site." [Online]. Available: http://www.fedex.com/.
9. "AWS Developer Forums." [Online]. Available: https://forums.aws.amazon.com.
10. "Amazon Web Services Developer Community : problem retrieving image location," 02-Nov-2008. [Online]. Available: http://developer.amazonwebservices.com/connect/thread.jspa?messageID=43937&#43937.
11. "PayPal X Developer Network." [Online]. Available: https://www.x.com/.
12. "developerFusion Discussion Forum." [Online]. Available: http://www.developerfusion.com/forum/thread/54751/.
13. "Design by Contract for Web Services | MyArch." [Online]. Available: http://myarch.com/design-by-contract-for-web-services.
14. W. T. Tsai, R. Paul, Y. Wang, C. Fan, and D. Wang, "Extending WSDL to facilitate Web services testing," in *7th IEEE International Symposium on High Assurance Systems Engineering, 2002. Proceedings*, 2002, pp. 171–172.
15. A. Bansal, K. Patel, G. Gupta, B. Raghavachari, E. Harris, and J. C. Staves, "Towards Intelligent Services: A Case Study in Chemical Emergency Response," presented at the ICWS 2005, 2005.
16. Z. Shelby, K. Hartke, and C. Bormann, "The Constrained Application Protocol (CoAP)." [Online]. Available: https://tools.ietf.org/html/rfc7252. [Accessed: 13-Jul-2015].
17. M. Barnett, K. R. M. Leino, and W. Schulte, "The Spec# Programming System: An Overview," in *Construction and Analysis of Safe, Secure, and Interoperable Smart Devices*, G. Barthe, L. Burdy, M. Huisman, J.-L. Lanet, and T. Muntean, Eds. Springer Berlin Heidelberg, 2005, pp. 49–69.
18. "Web Services Architecture," 2004. [Online]. Available: http://www.w3.org/TR/ws-arch/.
19. G. F. Coulouris, J. Dollimore, and T. Kindberg, *Distributed systems: concepts and design*. Addison-Wesley Longman, 2005.

I. Saleh, *Formalizing Data-Centric Web Services*, Web-Scale Workflow and Analytics, DOI 10.1007/978-3-319-24678-9

20. W. Frakes, L. Latour, and T. Wheeler, "Descriptive and Prescriptive Aspects of the 3C Model-SETA Working Group Summary," 1990.
21. "Common Object Request Broker Architecture (CORBA)," *Common Object Request Broker Architecture (CORBA)*. [Online]. Available: http://www.omg.org/corba/.
22. S. Torma, J. Villstedt, V. Lehtinen, I. Oliver, and V. Luukkala, "Semantic Web Services—A SURVEY," Technical Report published by Laboratory of Software Technology, Helsinki University of Technology, 2008.
23. B. W. Wah, *Wiley Encyclopedia of Computer Science and Engineering*, 1st ed. Wiley-Interscience, 2009.
24. J. M. Wing, "A Specifier's Introduction to Formal Methods," *Computer*, vol. 23, no. 9, pp. 8, 10–22, 24, Sep. 1990.
25. C. A. R. Hoare, "An Axiomatic Basis for Computer Programming," *Communications of the ACM*, vol. 12, no. 10, pp. 576–580, 1969.
26. G. T. Leavens, Y. Cheon, C. Clifton, C. Ruby, and D. R. Cok, "How the Design of JML Accommodates both Runtime Assertion Checking and Formal Verification," *Science of Computer Programming*, vol. 55, no. 1–3, pp. 185–208, Mar. 2005.
27. C. Flanagan, K. R. M. Leino, M. Lillibridge, G. Nelson, J. B. Saxe, and R. Stata, "Extended Static Checking for Java," 2002, pp. 234–245.
28. G. Kulczycki, "Tako: specification," 2009. [Online]. Available: http://www.nvc.vt.edu/gregwk/tako/specification.html.
29. Wayne Heym, "Computer Program Verification: Improvements for Human Reasoning," PhD Dissertation, The Ohio State University, 1995.
30. T. Haerder and A. Reuter, "Principles of transaction-oriented database recovery," *ACM Computing Surveys (CSUR)*, vol. 15, no. 4, pp. 287–317, 1983.
31. P. Hrastnik, "Integration of Transaction Management in Web Service Orchestrations," PhD Dissertation, Vienna University of Technology, Faculty of Informatics, Vienna, Austria, 2006.
32. D. Kaye, *Loosely Coupled: The Missing Pieces of Web Services*, 1st ed. RDS Press, 2003.
33. F. Baader, D. Calvanese, D. L. McGuinness, D. Nardi, and P. F. Patel-Schneider, *The Description Logic Handbook: Theory, Implementation, and Applications, 2nd Edition*, 2nd ed. Cambridge University Press, 2007.
34. R. Vaculin, H. Chen, R. Neruda, and K. Sycara, "Modeling and Discovery of Data Providing Services," Los Alamitos, CA, USA, 2008, vol. 0, pp. 54–61.
35. S. Lamparter, S. Luckner, and S. Mutschler, "Formal Specification of Web Service Contracts for Automated Contracting and Monitoring," 2007, p. 63.
36. "Web Services Policy Framework," *Web Services Policy Framework*, 09-Mar-2006. [Online]. Available: http://www.ibm.com/developerworks/library/specification/ws-polfram/.
37. "Extracting Functional and Non-Functional Contracts from Java Classes and Enterprise Java Beans." [Online]. Available: http://www.cs.kent.ac.uk/events/conf/2004/wads/DSN-WADS2004/Papers/milanovic.pdf.
38. F. Curbera, "Component Contracts in Service-Oriented Architectures," *Computer*, vol. 40, no. 11, pp. 74–80, Nov. 2007.
39. N. Chudasma and S. Chaudhary, "Service Composition using Service Selection with WS-Agreement," 2009, p. 21.
40. F. Raimondi, J. Skene, and W. Emmerich, "Efficient Online Monitoring of Web-Service SLAs," 2008, p. 170.
41. R. Souto, "On the Formal Specification and Derivation of Relational Database Applications," PhD Dissertation, University of Glasgow, 1994.
42. K. Bhattacharya, C. Gerede, R. Hull, R. Liu, and J. Su, "Towards Formal Analysis of Artifact-Centric Business Process Models," *Business Process Management*, pp. 288–304, 2007.
43. C. Gerede and J. Su, "Specification and verification of artifact behaviors in business process models," *Service-Oriented Computing–ICSOC 2007*, pp. 181–192, 2007.
44. A. Deutsch, R. Hull, F. Patrizi, and V. Vianu, "Automatic verification of data-centric business processes," 2009.

45. A. Deutsh and V. Vianu, "WAVE: Automatic Verification of Data-Driven Web Services," 2008, vol. 31 (3), pp. 35–39.

46. "OASIS Business Transaction Protocol." [Online]. Available: http://www.oasis-open.org/committees/tc_home.php?wg_abbrev=business-transaction.

47. "OASIS Web Services Transaction (WS-TX)," *http://www.oasis-open.org/committees/tc_home.php?wg_abbrev=ws-tx*, 2009. [Online]. Available: http://www.oasis-open.org/committees/tc_home.php?wg_abbrev=ws-tx.

48. "OASIS Web Services Business Activity (WS-Business Activity)," *http://docs.oasis-open.org/ws-tx/wstx-wsba-1.1-spec-pr-01.pdf*, 2006.

49. I. Saleh, "Formal Specification and Verification of Data-Centric Web Services," PhD Dissertation, Virginia Polytechnic Institute and State University, 2012.

50. I. Saleh, G. Kulczycki, and M. B. Blake, "Demystifying Data-Centric Web Services," *Internet Computing, IEEE*, vol. 13, no. 5, pp. 86–90, 2009.

51. I. Saleh, G. Kulczycki, and M. Blake, "A Reusable Model for Data-Centric Web Services," in *Formal Foundations of Reuse and Domain Engineering*, 2009, pp. 288–297.

52. I. Saleh, G. Kulczycki, M. B. Blake, and Y. Wei, "Static Detection of Implementation Errors Using Formal Code Specification," in *Software Engineering and Formal Methods*, R. M. Hierons, M. G. Merayo, and M. Bravetti, Eds. Springer Berlin Heidelberg, 2013, pp. 197–211.

53. I. Saleh, M. B. Blake, and G. Kulczycki, "Towards the Implementation of Bug-Free Database Applications: A Formal Approach," presented at the SIGMOD Workshop on Reliable Data Services and Systems (RDSS), 2014.

54. I. Saleh, G. Kulczycki, and M. B. Blake, "Formal Specification and Verification of Transactional Service Composition," presented at the 2011 IEEE World Congress on Services (SERVICES), 2011, pp. 474–481.

55. I. Saleh, G. Kulczycki, M. B. Blake, and Y. Wei, "Formal Methods for Data-Centric Web Services: From Model to Implementation," in *Proceedings of the IEEE International Conference on Web Services (ICWS'13)*, 2013, pp. 332–339.

56. G. Vossen, "On Formal Models for Object-Oriented Databases," *SIGPLAN OOPS Mess.*, vol. 6, no. 3, pp. 1–19, 1995.

57. E. F. Codd, *The Relational Model for Database Management: Version 2*. Addison-Wesley Longman Publishing Co., Inc., 1990.

58. C. J. Date, *An Introduction to Database Systems*, 8th ed. Addison Wesley, 2003.

59. G. Fisher, "Formal Specification Examples," 2007. [Online]. Available: http://users.csc.cal-poly.edu/~gfisher/classes/308/doc/ref-man/formal-spec-examples.html.

60. H. Kilov, "From Semantic to Object-Oriented Data Modeling," presented at the Systems Integration, 1990. Systems Integration '90., Proceedings of the First International Conference on, 1990, pp. 385–393.

61. "Introducing Express Checkout - PayPal," 2009. [Online]. Available: https://cms.paypal.com/us/cgi-bin/?cmd=_render-content&content_ID=developer/e_howto_api_EC GettingStarted.

62. Y. Cheon, G. Leavens, M. Sitaraman, and S. Edwards, "Model variables: cleanly supporting abstraction in design by contract: Research Articles," *Software -Practice & Experience*, vol. 35, no. 6, pp. 583–599, 2005.

63. M. Sitaraman, S. Atkinson, G. Kulczycki, B. W. Weide, T. J. Long, P. Bucci, W. Heym, S. Pike, and J. E. Hollingsworth, "Reasoning about software-component behavior," in *Software Reuse: Advances in Software Reusability*, Springer, 2000, pp. 266–283.

64. P. Chalin, J. R. Kiniry, G. T. Leavens, and E. Poll, "Beyond Assertions: Advanced Specification and Verification with JML and ESC/Java2," in *Formal Methods for Components and Objects*, vol. 4111, F. S. Boer, M. M. Bonsangue, S. Graf, and W.-P. Roever, Eds. Berlin, Heidelberg: Springer Berlin Heidelberg, 2006, pp. 342–363.

65. W. F. Ogden, M. Sitaraman, B. W. Weide, and S. H. Zweben, "The RESOLVE Framework and Discipline: a Research Synopsis," *SIGSOFT Software Engineering Notes*, vol. 19, no. 4, pp. 23–28, 1994.

66. "RESOLVE Web Interface," *http://resolve.cs.clemson.edu/demo/*. [Online]. Available: http://resolve.cs.clemson.edu/demo/.
67. J. R. Kiniry, A. E. Morkan, and B. Denby, "Soundness and Completeness Warnings in ESC/Java2," 2006, p. 24.
68. T. Nipkow, L. C. Paulson, and M. Wenzel, *Isabelle/HOL: a proof assistant for higher-order logic*, vol. 2283. Springer, 2002.
69. G. Klein, K. Elphinstone, G. Heiser, J. Andronick, D. Cock, P. Derrin, D. Elkaduwe, K. Engelhardt, R. Kolanski, M. Norrish, and others, "seL4: Formal Verification of an OS Kernel," 2009, pp. 207–220.
70. D. Chakraborty and A. Joshi, "Dynamic Service Composition: State-of-the-Art and Research Directions," Department of Computer Science and Electrical Engineering, University of Maryland, TR-CS-01-19, 2001.
71. B. Limthanmaphon and Y. Zhang, "Web Service Composition Transaction Management," Dunedin, New Zealand, 2004, pp. 171–179.
72. "The Java Modeling Language (JML) Home Page." [Online]. Available: http://www.eecs.ucf.edu/~leavens/JML/index.shtml.
73. K. R. M. Leino, "Dafny: an automatic program verifier for functional correctness," in *Proceedings of the 16th international conference on Logic for programming, artificial intelligence, and reasoning*, Berlin, Heidelberg, 2010, pp. 348–370.
74. M. Barnett, B.-Y. E. Chang, R. DeLine, B. Jacobs, and K. R. M. Leino, "Boogie: A Modular Reusable Verifier for Object-Oriented Programs," in *Formal Methods for Components and Objects*, F. S. de Boer, M. M. Bonsangue, S. Graf, and W.-P. de Roever, Eds. Springer Berlin Heidelberg, 2006, pp. 364–387.
75. L. De Moura and N. Bjørner, "Z3: an efficient SMT solver," in *Proceedings of the Theory and practice of software, 14th international conference on Tools and algorithms for the construction and analysis of systems*, Berlin, Heidelberg, 2008, pp. 337–340.
76. "JML Reference Manual." [Online]. Available: http://www.eecs.ucf.edu/~leavens/JML/jml-refman/jmlrefman_toc.html.
77. C. T. Cook, H. Harton, S. Hampton, and M. Sitaraman, "Modular Verification of Generic Components Using a Web-Integrated Environment," School of Computing, Clemson University, Clemson, SC, Technical Report RSRG-11-03, 2011.
78. "RESOLVE Tutorial." [Online]. Available: http://www.cs.clemson.edu/group/resolve/tutor/.
79. H. Smith, H. Harton, D. Frazier, R. Mohan, and M. Sitaraman, "Generating Verified Java Components through RESOLVE," in *Proceedings of the 11th International Conference on Software Reuse: Formal Foundations of Reuse and Domain Engineering*, Berlin, Heidelberg, 2009, pp. 11–20.
80. M. Sitaraman, B. Adcock, J. Avigad, D. Bronish, P. Bucci, D. Frazier, H. M. Friedman, H. Harton, W. Heym, J. Kirschenbaum, J. Krone, H. Smith, and B. W. Weide, "Building a Push-Button RESOLVE Verifier: Progress and Challenges," *Formal Aspects of Computing*, vol. 23, pp. 607–626, 2011.
81. "Dafny @ RiSE4fun - A Language and Program Verifier for Functional Correctness @ RiSE4fun - from Microsoft Research." [Online]. Available: http://www.riseforfun.com/Dafny.
82. "The Java Modeling Language (JML) Download Page." [Online]. Available: http://www.eecs.ucf.edu/~leavens/JML//download.shtml.
83. "OpenJml – jmlspecs." [Online]. Available: http://sourceforge.net/apps/trac/jmlspecs/wiki/OpenJml.
84. P. Chalin, P. R. James, J. Lee, and G. Karabotsos, "Towards an industrial grade IVE for Java and next generation research platform for JML," *International Journal on Software Tools for Technology Transfer (STTT)*, pp. 1–18, 2010.
85. M. Fähndrich, M. Barnett, and F. Logozzo, "Embedded contract languages," in *Proceedings of the 2010 ACM Symposium on Applied Computing*, New York, NY, USA, 2010, pp. 2103–2110.
86. J. Madhavan, D. Ko, Ł. Kot, V. Ganapathy, A. Rasmussen, and A. Halevy, "Google's Deep Web crawl," *Proc. VLDB Endow.*, vol. 1, no. 2, pp. 1241–1252, 2008.

87. K. Marriott and P. Stuckey, *Programming with Constraints: An Introduction*. The MIT Press, 1998.
88. J. M. Voas and G. McGraw, *Software Fault Injection: Inoculating Programs Against Errors*. John Wiley & Sons, 1998.
89. A. Derezińska, "Advanced Mutation Operators Applicable in C# Programs," in *Software Engineering Techniques: Design for Quality*, 2007, pp. 283–288.
90. Yue Jia and M. Harman, "An Analysis and Survey of the Development of Mutation Testing," *IEEE Transactions on Software Engineering*, vol. 37, no. 5, pp. 649–678, Oct. 2011.
91. R. A. DeMillo, D. S. Guindi, W. M. McCracken, A. J. Offutt, and K. N. King, "An extended overview of the Mothra software testing environment," presented at the Proceedings of the Second Workshop on Software Testing, Verification, and Analysis, 1988, 1988, pp. 142–151.
92. A. Derezinska and A. Szustek, "Tool-Supported Advanced Mutation Approach for Verification of C# Programs," presented at the Third International Conference on Dependability of Computer Systems, 2008. DepCos-RELCOMEX '08, 2008, pp. 261–268.
93. A. Derezinska, "Quality Assessment of Mutation Operators Dedicated for C# Programs," presented at the Sixth International Conference on Quality Software, 2006. QSIC 2006, 2006, pp. 227–234.
94. K. R. M. Leino and R. Monahan, "Automatic Verification of Textbook Programs that Use Comprehensions," presented at the ECOOP Workshop, Berlin, Germany, 2007.
95. E. W. Dijkstra, W. H. J. Feijen, and J. Sterringa, *A Method of Programming*, 1st English Ed. Addison-Wesley, 1988.
96. J. M. Voas and G. McGraw, *Software Fault Injection: Inoculating Programs Against Errors*. John Wiley & Sons, 1998.
97. "Book Rental System (C#.Net Windows Application)." [Online]. Available: http://www.dot-netspider.com/projects/974-Book-Rental-System-C-Net-Windows-Application.aspx.
98. G. T. Leavens and Y. Cheon, "Design by Contract with JML," *ftp://ftp.cs.iastate.edu/pub/leavens/JML/jmldbc.pdf*, 2006.
99. "Amazon Press Releases," *Amazon Press Releases*, Jan-2015. [Online]. Available: http://phx.corporate-ir.net/phoenix.zhtml?c=176060&p=irol-newsArticle&ID=2011466.
100. R. Kneuper, "Limits of Formal Methods," *Formal Aspects of Computing*, vol. 9, no. 4, pp. 379–394, 1997.
101. Luqi and J. A. Goguen, "Formal Methods: Promises and Problems," *IEEE Software*, vol. 14, no. 1, pp. 73–85, Feb. 1997.
102. I. Saleh and K. Nagi, "HadoopMutator: A Cloud-Based Mutation Testing Framework," presented at the 14th International Conference on Software Reuse (ICSR'15), FL, 2015, pp. 172–187.
103. *Apache™ Hadoop®*. [Online]. Available: https://hadoop.apache.org/.
104. K. Taneja, Y. Zhang, and T. Xie, "MODA: automated test generation for database applications via mock objects," 2010, pp. 289–292.

Printed in the United States
By Bookmasters